BULLY FREE at WORK

Bully Free at Work

WHAT YOU CAN DO TO **STOP** WORKPLACE BULLYING *NOW!*

VALERIE CADE, CSP

The Performance Curve International Publishing Co. ~ Calgary

Published by The Performance Curve International Corp.
Suite 356, 1500 - 14 Street NW
Calgary, Alberta   T3C 1C9
Canada
www.performancecurve.com

The Blog: www.bullyfreeatwork.com/blog
The Weekly Tip: www.howtohaveabullyfreeworkplace.com/weekly-tip.html
The Book: www.howtohaveabullyfreeworkplace.com

Disclaimer

The purpose of Bully Free at Work™ is to educate and empower individuals to eradicate workplace bullying. It outlines several options and their likely outcomes. However, it is up to each reader to decide which course of action is appropriate to his or her situation. No single course of action is recommended above others by the book and it is not claimed to be definitive or authoritative. Readers are encouraged to seek the services of a qualified, competent professional before moving to action.

Be assured that every effort has been taken to ensure the accuracy and integrity of the material presented in this book. The author, her agents and her employees, however, have neither liability nor responsibility to any person or entity with respect to any loss or damage caused or alleged to be caused directly or indirectly by the information the book contains.

**The Performance Curve International Publishing Co.
© 2008, 2011, 2013 Calgary Alberta Canada**

All rights reserved. No part of this publication may be reproduced, stored in a retrieval system, or transmitted in any form or by any means, electronic, mechanical, photocopying, recording, or otherwise, without the prior written permission of Performance Curve International Corp.

Printed in Canada.

Table of Contents

Read Me First!   1

Chapter 1–
Workplace Bullying: What Everyone Must Know   3

   1. Workplace Bullying Defined   3
   2. Why Do We Tolerate Workplace Bullying?   6
   3. How Common Is Workplace Bullying?   7
   4. Is Workplace Bullying the Same As Harassment?   8
   5. Workplace Bullying Hurts People   9
   6. Workplace Bullying Hurts Organizations   10
   7. Workplace Bullying and Its Effects Can Be Stopped   13
   8. Who This Book Is For   13
      • Targets of Bullying   13
      • Counselors, Social Workers and Life Coaches   14
      • Lawyers   14

Chapter 2 – Are You Being Bullied?   19

   1. What Is Bullying?   19
      • How to Tell If It's Bullying   20
        Self-Test: Are You Being Bullied?   23
   2. Workplace Bullying: The Differences Between Men and Women   25
   3. Wonder Why the Bully Is a Bully? Patterns Set in Childhood May Tell Us More   26
   4. Understanding What Motivates a Bully   28
   5. Envy: The Main Drive Behind the Bully   33
   6. Types of Bullies   35
      • A: Arrogant Bullies   36
      • B: Manipulative Bullies   37
      • C: Dictator Bullies   39
      • D: Victim Bullies   41
      • E: Suspicious Bullies   43

7. How Serious Is Bullying? 45
8. The Facts You Need to Know About Workplace Bullying 46
9. Behavior That Gets Rewarded Gets Repeated 48
10. Common Bullying Tactics 49
    - Bullying Tactic: Verbal Abuse 49
    - Bullying Tactic: Exclusion 54
    - Bullying Tactic: Unfairness or "Crazy-Making" 55
    - Bullying Tactic: Lack of Clarity 58

Chapter 3 – Why Me? 61

1. Who Do Bullies Target? 63
   - Natural Targets 63
   - Un-Empowered Targets 64
   - "Different" Targets 65
   - Targets of Whom the Bully Is Jealous 65
   - Targets Who Threaten the Bully's Control 66
   - Situational Targets 67
2. Are You Vulnerable to Bullying? 68
   Self-Test: Are You Wearing a Bull's Eye on Your Back? 69
3. The Bullying Cycle 71
4. Steps an Organization Can Take to Be Bully Free at Work ™ and to Create a Respectful Workplace 76

Chapter 4 – Effects of Workplace Bullying 79

1. Symptomatic Effects of Being Bullied 79
2. The Full Price of Bullying 84

Chapter 5 – So What Can You Do? – First Steps 89

1. Four-Pronged Response to Workplace Bullying 89
   - State the Problem 90
   - Acknowledge the Bullying 90

- Understand How Bullying Affects You 93
- Admit Your Anger 95
- Remind Yourself That It Is About the Bully 95
    Assignment: Stating the Problem 96
2. Protect Yourself 98
    - Bully-Proof Yourself 98
    - Document the Bullying 99
    - Protect Your Health 101
    - Get Support Right Away 102
    - Know That You Will Get Through This 103

Chapter 6 – Take Care of Yourself 107

1. Health and Wellness 107
    - The Wellness Wheel 108
        Assignment: The Wellness Wheel 109
        Assignment: Action Plan to Improve Physical Health 110
2. Take Care of Your Physical Health 110
3. Manage Your Stress Level 111
4. Steps to Reducing Stress 114
    - Nurture Yourself 114
        Assignment: Identify Calming Activities 114
    - Have Some Fun 115
    - Meditation and Prayer 116
    - Regulate Your Breathing 116
    - Avoid "Multi-Tasking" 117
    - Put a Halt to Negative Self-Talk 118
        Exercise: Reframing Negative Thoughts 119
5. Enlist Support 121

Chapter 7 – Empower Yourself 123

1. Assemble Your Support Team 125
    - "Can We Talk?" 128
2. Build Your Self-Esteem 131
    Exercise: Rosenberg Self-Esteem Scale 132

	• Self-Esteem and Personal Responsibility	134
	• Focus on Your Strengths	135
	Assignment: Identify Your Strengths	137
	• Improve Your Options	139
3.	Learn How to Make Good Decisions	139
	• Three Steps to Good Decisions	140
	Assignment: Decision-Making Step #1	
	— Identify Your Options	141
4.	Learn How to Assert Yourself	142

Chapter 8 – Handling the Bully   145

1.	Things You Can Do Now to Stop the Impact of Bullying	146
	• Why Should You Be the One to Change?	148
2.	Minor Bullying	148
3.	Moderate-Level Bullying	149
	• Enlisting Support	151
	• Speaking Up to the Boss: The Top Fears	151
	• Asserting Yourself	152
	Self-Test: How Assertive Are You?	154
	• The Process of Becoming Assertive	156
	• Which Came First: The Behavior or the Belief?	157
	Assignment: Responding Assertively	158
	• Learning to Take Control of Your Life	159
	Assignment: Daily Debriefing	160
	Asserting Yourself with the Bully: What to Expect	160
	• Considering How to Approach the Bully	162
	• Confronting the Bully Is HARD	165
	• How to Talk to the Bully: A Classy, Crucial Conversation That Counts	168
	• After the Confrontation	171
4.	Severe Bullying	171
	• Deciding Whether or Not to Get Help in Your Organization	172
	• Deciding Whether to Stay or Go	173

5. Prepare to Leave, Even If You Don't 173
   • What Are You Afraid Of? 173
   • Great Decision Making 175
      Assignment: Decision-Making Step #2
         — Evaluating Your Options 176
      Assignment: Decision-Making Step #3
         — Choose an Option 178

Chapter 9 – The Top 21 Tips 181

1. Ask Yourself: Are You Watering Seeds or Weeds? 182
2. "Fair" and "Unfair" Conversations: Know the Difference for Increased Power 183
3. What Do You Do with Your Feelings? 184
4. How Anger and Frustration Are Expressed: Heavy Control 186
5. How Anger and Frustration Are Expressed: Passive Control 187
6. What Will You Do with Your Anger and Frustration? 189
7. Say What You Mean and Mean What You Say 190
8. Responding to Discounting 192
9. Avoiding the Issue: Keeping You Powerless 194
10. Sarcasm – It's *Not* Funny 195
11. Mind Reading 196
12. Being Interrupted 198
13. Mirroring 199
14. Make Requests 200
15. Respond with "I Understand" or "I See" 200
16. Gunny-Sacking 200
17. Cold-Shoulder Treatment 201
18. Acting Like You've Made an Unreasonable Request 201
19. What to Do When the Bully Attacks You with Untrue Accusations 202
20. Short, Simple Come-Backs to Use with Bullies 204

21. How to Change Workplace Bullying: You Really
    Can Have Something Better!   205

Chapter 10 – Bully Free At Work™: What Employers Can Do About Workplace Bullying   209

1. What Makes an Organization Vulnerable
   to Bullying?   209
2. Workplace Bullying: The Aftermath   210
   - Clarify and communicate organization's values   214
   - Use managers as role models   214
   - Develop open communication between
     management and employees   215
   - Provide a complaint process   215
   - Train managers and employees about bullying   216
   - Support interpersonal skills training for employees   216
   - Punish bullies   216
   - Don't hire bullies   216
   - Conduct an employee survey   217
4. Generating a "Bully Free At Work ™" Policy in
   Your Workplace   217

Conclusion   223

Appendix: Self-Tests, Assignments and Exercises   227

1. Self-Test: Are You Being Bullied?   228
2. Self-Test: Are You Wearing a Bull's Eye on
   Your Back?   230
3. Self-Test: How Bullying Is Affecting You   232
4. Assignment: Stating the Problem   235
5. Exercise: Casting Yourself Forward One Year   237
6. Exercise: Wellness Wheel   238
7. Assignment: Action Plan to Improve
   Physical Health   238
8. Assignment: Identifying Calming Activities   239

9. Exercise: Reframing Negative Thoughts	240
10. Assignment: Action Plan to Reduce Stress	241
11. Assignment: Identifying Your Support Team	242
12. Exercise: Rosenberg Self-Esteem Scale	243
13. Assignment: Identify Your Strengths	244
14. Assignment: Decision-Making Step #1 —Identify Your Options	246
15. Self-Test: How Assertive Are You?	247
16. Assignment: Responding Assertively	249
17. Assignment: Daily Debriefing	250
18. Assignment: Preparing to Leave	250
19. Assignment: Decision-Making Step #2 —Evaluating Your Options	252
20. Assignment: Decision-Making Step #3 —Choose an Option	254

Bibliography   255

About the Author   257

Read Me First!

Congratulations on your decision to read Bully Free at Work™. You are joining many people throughout the world in a quest to stop workplace bullying; and to each person reading this book, I wish you the empowerment and joy you deserve.

Before you start reading, I recommend:

1. To get comfortable and to treat your reading time as a gift to yourself.

2. Whether you have been bullied, know of a bully or perhaps display bullying tendencies, this book will serve as a resource for you for years to come. If you are in a leadership role responsible for morale and productivity, this book will give you the support you need to address workplace bullying with more ease. Know that you have a community of people out there pulling for your every success.

I want to thank the many clients who have entrusted me with their confidence in sharing their experiences. Also, many thanks to all the staff at Bully Free at Work™ – you are World Class. And a very special thank you to Pat Flynn, Sheila Rae and Celeste Peters for their passion and dedication. Without their talent and capabilities, this book would not have been possible.

Together we can stop workplace bullying. We are in your corner.

Sincerely,

Valerie Cade

Valerie Cade, CSP
Founder
Bully Free at Work

CHAPTER 1

Workplace Bullying: What Everyone Must Know

> ### Overview
>
> 1. Workplace Bullying Defined
> 2. Why Do We Tolerate Workplace Bullying?
> 3. How Common Is Workplace Bullying?
> 4. Is Workplace Bullying the Same As Harassment?
> 5. Workplace Bullying Hurts People
> 6. Workplace Bullying Hurts Organizations Too
> 7. Workplace Bullying and Its Effects Can Be Stopped
> 8. Who This Book Is For

1. Workplace Bullying Defined

"I used to just love my job – I mean love it. The people in the department and the company were all great. As soon as Paul transferred in, things started going downhill. I swear he seemed to have it in for me from the very first second. Right away he started making sarcastic remarks to me. He sent me harassing emails, asking why didn't I 'get it', that I didn't have the experience to make the recommendations I was suggesting; saying that no one paid any attention to me; constantly telling me I should review this memo or that memo so that I would 'come across as more intelligent'. He conducted meetings, 'forgetting' to tell me about them. He

3

even spread lies, saying that my personal life was interfering with getting my job done...

"Suddenly, my whole work world has turned upside down. It seems like, no matter what I do, it's never good enough. I can barely sleep, I'm exhausted, I'm a nervous wreck, and I'm on edge. I dread going to work every day. It's become so bad, I'm on anti-depressants. Honestly, I feel like I'm going crazy. What happened? I just want things to be the way they were..."

Does this sound like something you've ever experienced, or maybe are going through now? If you're being bullied, or aren't sure whether or not you're being bullied, and you don't know what to do about it, this book was written for you.

Many of us think of bullying as a childhood behavior, the playground bully who picks on other kids, stealing their lunch money, playing cruel jokes, even beating them up. Even those of us who have been or *are right now* being tormented by other adults may not realize that what we are experiencing is *bullying*. The playground bully has grown up – or, at least, he is now an adult – and his new playground is the workplace.

A question many people ask is: How do I know if I am being bullied, or if I am dealing with a difficult person—what is the difference? Both situations are unfortunate and both carry an atmosphere of disrespect. Workplace bullying, however, is repeated, deliberate, disrespectful behavior by one or more people toward another for their own gratification, which in turn harms the target. Bullying is unreasonable behavior, which you most often cannot negotiate. Negotiation and change are more likely to occur with difficult people. Bullying is deliberate, not accidental. Bullying is always disrespectful with intent. Bullying results in gratification for the bully, where the target feels severely disrespected. Difficult people are not necessarily out to harm another; they are out to protect their own needs. Therefore, if you can reason with a difficult person in order to show good will for their needs, they may change. A bully will not change. Ask yourself, Is this person deliberate in trying to cause harm…repeatedly? If so, it is workplace bullying.

> Bullying is repeated, deliberate, disrespectful behavior by one or more people toward another for their own gratification, which harms the target.

According to the online encyclopedia, Wikipedia, "Workplace bullying, like childhood bullying, is the tendency of individuals or groups to use aggressive or unreasonable behavior to achieve their ends. When perpetrated by a group, it is often called mobbing. Unlike the more physical form of schoolyard bullying, workplace bullies often operate within the established rules and policies of their organization and their society. For instance, a workplace bully might use the office's "rumour mill" to circulate a lie about a co-worker. An employee who dislikes a co-worker for personal reasons may incessantly criticize everything that co-worker does. Such actions are not necessarily illegal and may not even be against the organization's regulations. However, the damage

> Unlike schoolyard bullies, workplace bullies often operate within the established rules and policies of their organization.
>
> What does this say about the organization?

they cause, both to the targeted employee and to workplace morale, is obvious."[1]

Often, the target of bullying will, in an effort to avoid a problem, try to accommodate or appease the bully. The target might, for instance, agree with her, begin submitting to her demands, remain silent rather than disagreeing with her, or just avoid her. Ironically, this fuels the bullying behavior because the bully gets what she wants and she sees the target as being weak.

2. Why Do We Tolerate Workplace Bullying?

Two major risk factors for illness and injury are:

1. Hostility (as used by the bully).
2. Loneliness (as often experienced by the target).

If our health is at risk, why would we tolerate bullying?

There are 3 primary reasons:

1. We feel it is socially unacceptable to "push back";

2. The fear that if we push back, will we really win, or will it make matters worse and provoke the bully even more?

3. As we are being thwarted, we start to forget that we have rights, needs and wants. Instead we start to focus on what the bully is saying and demanding of us, rather than taking steps to bully proof ourselves. We react to the bully's demands and lose a vision of what we want and need, leaving us fearful and afraid as opposed to secure and empowered.

---

[1] http://en.wikipedia.org/wiki/Workplace_bullying

3. How Common Is Workplace Bullying?

So, just how common is bullying in the workplace? Very common. Workplace bullying has been taken seriously in the United Kingdom, parts of Europe, Australia and Canada since the 1980s, but not until the 1990s has it been identified as a serious problem in the United States. However, reported or not, workplace bullying occurs in <u>every</u> country in the world.

The International Labour Organization (ILO) cited research conducted in the UK that found that 53 percent of employees had been victims of workplace bullying and that 78 percent had witnessed workplace bullying.[2] In a press release dated July 1998, the ILO stated that "Workplace bullying is one of the fastest growing complaints of workplace violence," describing workplace bullying as "offensive behavior through vindictive, cruel, malicious or humiliating attempts to undermine an individual or groups of employees…"

Wikipedia states that "Statistics show that bullying is three times as prevalent as illegal discrimination and at least 1,600 times as prevalent as workplace violence. Statistics also show that while only one employee in every 10,000 becomes a victim of workplace violence, one in six experiences bullying at work. Bullying is also far more common than sexual harassment and verbal abuse."[3]

---

2   International Labour Organization "Violence on the job…a global problem." Press release, Geneva, Washington, D.C.: 20 July 1998.
3   http://en.wikipedia.org/wiki/Bullying#Workplace.

4. Is Workplace Bullying the Same As Harassment?

Is harassment the same as bullying? Yes. The late Tim Field, an expert about the problem of bullying, explained, "Bullying is, I believe, the underlying behavior and thus the common denominator of harassment, discrimination, stalking and abuse. What varies is the focus of expression of the behavior. For instance, a harasser or discriminator focuses on race or gender or disability. Bullies focus on competence and popularity which at present are not covered by employment legislation."[4]

Harassment and bullying generally refer to the same behavior: persistent, unwelcome, aggressive behavior imposed on a person by another, whether or not it is blatant or subtle, and whether or not it is inspired by the gender, ethnicity, sexual orientation, the age of the target, some other specific characteristic (such as disability), or not. Usually the intent is hostile and mean-spirited; intended to make the target feel miserable. In the case of sexual harassment, the behavior disregards the target's personal dignity and is often intended to be outright demeaning.

According to Harvey Hornstein, author of *Brutal Bosses and Their Prey*, (1996), a staggering 90% of the workforce suffers from abuse at the hands of their boss some time during their careers and, on any given day, 20% of employees are being bullied by their bosses.[5]

Bullying is especially prevalent in the helping professions, such as nursing and social services. It's easy for the bully

---

[4] Vaknin, Sam, Ph.D. "Bully At Work: An Interview with Tim Field." The Global Politician, May 28, 2005.

[5] Hornstein, H. Ph. D. Brutal Bosses and Their Prey. New York: Riverhead Books, 1996. p. xiii.

to find many who fit the bully target profile *(please see Chapter 3, **Why Me?**) but the environment itself fosters cooperation, sympathy and patience and, therefore, may not be as confrontive to bullying behavior as is needed.

5. Workplace Bullying Hurts People

Anyone who has been the victim of bullying can testify as to its painful, often debilitating effects. There is, at the very least, emotional hurt, embarrassment, confusion and increased stress. Usually though, the toll is far greater, with the target suffering extreme emotional pain, depression, intense anxiety, a complete inability to concentrate and function on the job, insomnia, headaches, stomach pains, increased blood pressure, and other physical and emotional problems. The effects can be devastating.

Many people also experience being bullied, or being abused at home. What is the difference between bullying and abuse? A workplace bully is disrespectful towards a target. An abusive person is disrespectful towards a victim.

> **A workplace bully is disrespectful towards a target.**
> **An abusive person is disrespectful towards a victim.**

In the workplace, for someone who is being bullied, they are called a target, rather than a victim. The word victim *implies* total helplessness. Ideally, in the workplace there can be policies and rules set forth to stop workplace bullying – a protection, if you will – rather than having the position of helplessness and no support as one may face in a personal situation. This is the ideal work situation in which the target can have a safe place in which to turn for support.

About 75% of people who are bullied tend to have some level of self-awareness, self-esteem and assertiveness to handle the bully and either not take it personally, and/or assert back with confidence. It is the remaining 25% of those people being bullied who suffer greatly; either the bullying was so severe, or the target had diminished coping skills.

6. Workplace Bullying Hurts Organizations

Bullying creates chaos in an organization. It is destructive and expensive. An obvious cost is the productivity of employees being bullied. Their work almost certainly will suffer. A previously high-performing employee may stop taking initiative, start making mistakes, not complete assignments, or be absent from work. His or her work safety habits may decline, while the number of conflicts with other employees goes up. Once a valuable asset, he or she may now be very low-performing, high maintenance; an accident waiting to happen, a law suit waiting to be filed.

The morale of other employees will also be affected, teamwork will diminish, and the workplace environment, once agreeable, cooperative and productive, is suddenly hostile. The best, most loyal employees will begin to leave. Safe work practices are compromised, there is more absenteeism, more conflicts in the work force, more theft. When loyalty goes away, resentment takes it place. So the organization is left with only the mediocre – and the bullies!

Not only will the company lose quality people, it won't be able to attract quality employees. Or, if it does, it won't be able to retain them when the new employees figure out what's going on.

Then of course there are the legal and financial risks. In the

UK, Australia, Canada and the US, as well as other countries in Europe and elsewhere around the world, employers are legally obligated to provide a safe and healthful environment for workers. Case law has long supported the premise that this includes the emotional and mental safety and health of employees. Some countries have only anti-discrimination and anti-harassment laws, while others have specific anti-bullying legislation. Bullying that has a discrimination or harassment component has the law on its side. For example, a white employee bullying a person of color, a male bullying a female, a heterosexual bullying a homosexual, an able-bodied person bullying a person with a disability, and so forth, can bring a separate and very large risk of legal and financial penalties. But what about the workplace bullying incidents that do not fall under discrimination or harassment? There are many situations of workplace bullying that fall in this category. Currently, government legislation is not prevalent, leaving many people unprotected. However, organizations can develop workplace bullying policies and work to activate them – this is a moral beginning.

What are the top consequences for an organization as a result of someone being bullied?

1. Good morale (a positive culture) is traded for a fearful culture where people become hesitant, less free and less open.

2. Teamwork will deteriorate into group-work or individual efforts.

3. The agreeable, cooperative and supportive environment becomes hostile, secretive and dead.

4. The best most loyal employees begin to leave.

5. Safe work practices are compromised.

6. Absenteeism, increase in sick days.

7. More indirect conflicts.

8. Loss of loyalty.

9. Increase in resentment.

10. Increase in theft, acting out and sabotage.

Many people ask: Can workplace bullying be stopped and prevented? The answer is: Yes.

1. The first step is an informed workforce. Information as to what workplace bullying is, how it occurs, who are likely to be targets and bullies, and systems and accountabilities in place to protect and create the kind of workplace culture that is respectful.

2. The second step is to empower employees to create and enforce workplace-bullying policies that protect a respectful workplace and hold employees accountable for bullying behavior.

Workplace bullying can be stopped, but it must not rest only on the target's shoulders to stop this behavior. Stopping workplace bullying is everyone's responsibility. Upper management must use their authority to ensure that a respectful workplace exists.

7. Workplace Bullying and Its Effects Can Be Stopped

I was inspired to write this book because so many people who attend my training seminars on empowerment, teamwork, assertiveness and communication have shared with me how much they identified with my description of the workplace bullying experience. After considerable research, I saw how prevalent workplace bullying actually is. I also saw how serious the need is for help and support for people being targeted by bullying behavior.

In this book, I will share with you how to stop the workplace bullying if that's possible; and, if it's not, how to protect yourself from the bullying. Part of what we'll discuss is why you are being targeted, how to be bully free at work, how to develop assertiveness skills if this is an issue for you, and how to rebuild the self-esteem that has been damaged by being bullied.

8. Who This Book Is For

Targets of Bullying

This book is primarily for those of you out there who are struggling with the experience of being bullied in the workplace, or maybe wonder if what is happening to you is in fact workplace bullying. I want to reassure you that you are not alone out there and you are not helpless in the face of this problem. You can reclaim your energy, love for your work, and self-esteem. As a matter of fact, I'll show you how you can achieve a more enjoyable work life and experience higher levels of self-confidence - you deserve to feel respected and supported.

My goal is to help you to be able to identify a workplace bully, understand why you're being targeted and learn how to be bully free at work. I also want to equip you with skills to cope effectively with workplace bullying, including protecting your health and your job, managing your stress level, asserting yourself, confronting the workplace bully, deciding whether to stay in your job or move on, and coming up with a solid exit strategy if you do decide to leave your job.

Counselors, Social Workers and Life Coaches

This book is also intended to help counselors, social workers and life coaches who have clients going through a workplace bullying experience. You might be their first line of defence. By identifying the workplace bullying behavior and hearing about the symptoms that your client is suffering, you will be able to recognize when workplace bullying is occurring, even if your client does not. I hope my work here will give you insight into your clients' subjective experience of being bullied, even if they themselves might not have the awareness to frame the experience as such.

Lawyers

For labour attorneys, I hope this work will help you recognize the challenges your client is being forced to navigate and, hopefully, also help you determine what corrective action or relief might be appropriate.

Supervisors, Managers and HR Professionals

Finally, I invite supervisors, managers and Human Resources professionals out there who sincerely care about your employees' well-being, to read this book as well. It will, perhaps, give you insight about what bullying looks like – and how it feels to the target. You'll also be better able to assess whether conditions in your department or organization encourage bullying and, if so, how to change that.

Throughout this book, you will notice that I switch back and forth between the male and female genders for both bullies and targets so as to most accurately portray the reality of bullying. Bullies and targets can be men or women.

To those of you who are suffering at the hands of a bully right now, know that you will get through this! And, what's more, you'll survive it while being true to your values, keeping your caring nature intact, and acquiring the courage to stand up for what you believe. You can emerge with new confidence, a healthy assertiveness that will serve you well in life. You can learn to express your feelings and opinions honestly and without apology; drawing upon courage you never knew you had. You can become wiser, but not cynical, ending up with a more accepting, loving view of human nature, yet not vulnerable to bullies.

As with any hardship, surviving a bullying experience can bring with it opportunities you never would have imagined. Perhaps you will emerge with a stronger sense of who you are, what you value and your self-worth. Of course you wouldn't willingly sign up to be bullied. Who would? But, if it's something that's already happening to you, at least take from the experience whatever benefits and opportunities it offers.

An example:

No sooner had Simon transferred into the department when Corey started to taunt him. Corey seemed to get a kick out of Simon's embarrassment and soon was calling him Simple Simon and playing little practical jokes on him. He particularly liked to heckle him in front of others, to Simon's great humiliation. A somewhat passive person who kept to himself, Simon tried to stay out of Corey's way but that wasn't really practical. Simon had always gotten along well with fellow employees and just couldn't understand what the problem was. Corey seemed to get meaner by the day. Simon went into a tailspin – he didn't know what to do. He was in crisis.

He began seeing a counselor to help him cope with the problem. First, she focused on his physical and emotional health, including his stress level, which was sky-high. She helped Simon establish some healthy routines and stress reduction techniques so that, before long, he was sleeping better again, eating well, and getting some exercise. They continued to work on stress reduction, as well as on building his self-esteem and developing a stronger support network (which included improving his communication skills). They also focused on assertiveness skills, and Simon even attended an assertiveness training workshop that his counselor recommended. Simon and his counselor did assertiveness role playing exercises based on the notes he kept describing encounters with Corey.

Slowly, Simon began standing up to Corey, not arguing with him or insulting him, but simply showing Corey that he was no longer intimidated or embarrassed by him. Simon stayed focused on doing his job well and neither avoided nor sought out interaction with Corey. It took a while, but eventually Corey became just another employee in the department to

Simon, not his favorite but not a problem, either. More importantly, though, Simon's self-esteem soared and he has developed a small circle of friends who have become an important part of his life. He still isn't the most self-assured guy in the world, but he asserts himself when an issue is important to him.

The effects of bullying don't have to exist at all. You *can* reclaim your sense of dignity, confidence and well-being.

Chapter 2

Are You Being Bullied?

Overview

1. What Is Bullying?
   Self-Test: Are You Being Bullied?
2. Workplace Bullying: The Differences Between Men and Women
3. Wonder Why the Bully Is a Bully? Patterns Set in Childhood May Tell Us More
4. Understanding What Motivates A Bully
5. Envy: The Main Drive Behind the Bully
6. Types of Bully Bosses
7. How Serious Is Bullying?
8. The Facts You Need to Know About Workplace Bullying
9. Behavior That Gets Rewarded Gets Repeated
10. Common Bullying Tactics

1. What Is Bullying?

All conflict in the workplace isn't bullying. An isolated incident does not constitute bullying because bullying is a pattern of repeated behavior. Unintentional insensitivity, though potentially hurtful, is not bullying because it is not deliberate. Ignoring a person may be rude but is not necessarily bullying unless the ignorer is going for a specific reaction. Bullying is repeated, deliberate, disrespectful behavior by one or more people toward another for their own gratification, and which harms the target.

> Bullying is repeated, deliberate, disrespectful behavior by one or more people toward another for their own gratification, which harms the target.

Author Andrea Adams believed that workplace bullying is one of the greatest sources of stress for employees, and that organizations are slow to recognize this.[6] Part of the apparent indifference to the phenomenon of bullying by employers is probably that bullying is seen as a childhood behavior and, therefore, not a serious issue in the adult world. Adams goes on to say that targets are expected to "not take any nonsense" and to "pull themselves together". Unless the behavior is certifiably illegal (such as sexual harassment or discrimination on the basis of, say, race), employers may just look at the problem as lack of assertiveness on the target's part, a personality conflict, or even a "style" difference. "What to a victim may seem to be a horrendous, stressful form of persecution," explains bullying researcher Peter Randall, "may be to the observer nothing more than two or more people who do not get on together."[7]

How to Tell If It's Bullying

Case Study: Sam (Surly)

You've been on the new job about three weeks. You felt unwelcome as soon as you were introduced to your new co-worker, Sam. He showed no enthusiasm to meet you and, after three weeks, he's no friendlier. In fact, he is abrupt and grouchy with you. He rarely says "Good morning" unless you

---

6   Adams, A. Bullying at Work. London: Virago, 1992.
7   Randall, P. Adult Bullying: Perpetrators and Victims. London/New York: Taylor & Francis, 1997, p. 9.

say it first (and usually not even then) and responds to your attempts at conversation with short answers, if at all. He makes little attempt to help you, even when it's obvious you need assistance. When you ask him a question related to the job, he looks impatient and gives you the bare minimum of information. The other day, he was almost yelling at you, saying "You've asked me that three times now – here, look it up yourself!" and handing you the procedure manual. He takes a coffee break with a few people who work down the hall and has not once invited you to join them. You often feel foolish, intimidated and isolated. And you're wondering if taking the job was a mistake and whether Sam is, indeed, a bully.

Probably not. It doesn't sound like Sam is a very pleasant person to work with but his behavior doesn't rise to the level of bullying. The behavior is repeated, which is one element of bullying. Although it is somewhat disrespectful and certainly is harming you, it really doesn't sound deliberate or for Sam's gratification, because it's doubtful Sam is even aware of his behavior, much less its effect on you. It's a fact of life that some people just aren't as cooperative, friendly and helpful as others. The good news here is that when dealing with a difficult person, he or she is usually unaware of how his or her behavior causes damage to others, and may be open to change if approached with care – more on this later!

Does that necessarily mean you should put up with this kind of behavior? No, of course not; especially if it is causing you a lot of stress. Things might improve as you and Sam get more used to one another. As you become more skilled in your job, you might choose to talk with Sam about the problem, or you might get to a point where you don't take this personally – it says more about Sam than you.

Case Study: Charlene (Churlish)

There was a general air of standoffishness when you first transferred into the department a few months ago and one of your new co-workers, Charlene, even refused to attend the meeting in which you were being introduced to the group. Your new co-workers were clearly sceptical of you, although most have warmed up considerably since then.

Except Charlene. No matter what you suggest, Charlene takes the opposing position. She is abrupt with you and often downright rude. In meetings, it seems like she challenges and contradicts you at every opportunity, making no attempt to disguise her dislike for you; in fact, she goes out of her way to show her disdain. You can tell she has made derogatory remarks to others in the company about you by subtle remarks that are made.

You have gone out of your way to be extra friendly and cooperative with Charlene, but she rebuffs your attempts. You even asked her if you had offended her in some way, to which she responded, "I don't have to like everyone at work." She doesn't answer your emails or phone calls and takes action without consulting you, even when it's in your area of responsibility. Last week, she wrote an email to the Executive Vice President, criticizing you harshly about your handling of a project, although she never registered any concern about it to you directly.

Charlene's behavior has been causing you constant stress and anxiety. Instead of focusing on the priorities you would normally attend to, you find yourself obsessing to avoid Charlene's wrath. It seems like you haven't won the credibility and cooperation that you usually do with your peers and you need in order to be effective in your job. So, would you call Charlene's behavior bullying?

Yes, definitely. It is repeated, deliberate and disrespectful, and it is harming you.

Self-Test: Are You Being Bullied?

Consider each of the questions in the self-test below and decide if you Strongly Agree, Somewhat Agree, Disagree, or Strongly Disagree. Then, circle the corresponding number.

Does the person you're having challenges with:	Strongly Agree	Agree	Somewhat Agree	Disagree	Strongly Disagree
1. Ignore you. Not say hello when you greet them. Not return phone calls or emails.	5	4	3	2	1
2. Dismiss what you're saying or "put you down" while alone or in the presence of others?	5	4	3	2	1
3. Sabotage you or make you look foolish, such as "forgetting" to tell you about meetings (or) if the person is your boss, set you up to fail by making impossible demands of you?	6	5	4	3	2
4. Spread rumours, lies and half-truths about you?	6	5	4	3	2
5. Frequently act impatient with you, treating you like you're incompetent?	5	4	3	2	1
6. Routinely blame and criticize you?	5	4	3	2	1

Does the person you're having challenges with:		Strongly Agree	Agree	Somewhat Disagree	Disagree	Strongly Disagree
7.	Try to intimidate you by interrupting, contradicting, glaring, acting forceful or giving you the silent treatment?	5	4	3	2	1
8.	Ridicule, insult or play tricks on you, especially in front of others?	6	5	4	3	2
9.	Always insist on getting their own way and never apologizing?	5	4	3	2	1
10.	Leave you out of social and work situations as opposed to inviting or including you?	6	5	4	3	2
	Total score = _____ (Possible total of 54)	Now add your score.				

Remember, workplace bullying can be tough to measure because of its subjectivity. Bullying occurs when a target experiences repeated disrespectful behavior. These are (some) of the top disrespectful behaviors experienced by targets and know there are more. This self-test is primarily designed to help you name and become more aware of any severity.

If your score is 24 or below, it doesn't look like you're being bullied. If your score is between 25 and 34, there are indications of bullying behavior. If your score is 35 or above, you are definitely being bullied.

2. Workplace Bullying: The Differences Between Men and Women

Bullies come in all shapes and sizes, and so do targets. There is no conclusive evidence that bullying or being bullied is dependent on gender, ethnicity, age or other demographic factors.

Who bullies more, men or women?

Men and women bully evenly. The general perception is that men bully more; but that may be because we still associate negative behavior with being more overt and aggressive, which is seen as a male tendency. Females tend to resort more to passive-aggressive forms of bullying.

The Workplace Bullying and Trauma Institute (WBTI) reported a 2000 survey indicating that women and men were just as likely to be bullies, although women were much more likely to be targets (77% of instances, compared to 23% for men).[8] Research conducted at the University of Manchester Institute of Science and Technology (UMIST), found that women and men were bullied at about the same rates.[9]

While there is conflicting research about whether or not women tend to be targeted by bullies more than men, women may, indeed, be more attractive targets. Why? Because in many societies, males are socialized to be competitive and aggressive while females are encouraged to be kind, patient, tolerant, sympathetic, and so forth. Made to order for a bully! Members of certain cultures may similarly be more vulnerable to bullying if, for instance, the culture places a high value on politeness and non-confrontation.

---

8   http://www.bullyinginstitute.org/bbstudies/worktrauma.html#who
9   Rayner, C., Hoel, H.; Cooper, C.L. Workplace Bullying. London/New York: Taylor & Francis, 2002, p. 28.

3. Wonder Why the Bully Is a Bully? Patterns Set in Childhood May Tell Us More

Nearly every study I have read about "Why Does Someone Bully?" indicates some level of childhood challenge.

When the bully becomes an adult, the difficulty is that they have not become aware of their childhood challenges in any way. In fact, what they have done is suppressed the challenges, resulting in a need.

Here are some childhood challenges that can result in suppression of feelings and emotions:

1. Being told, "I will love you if..." - conditional love. This causes instability in one's self esteem and self worth, with the child feeling like they have to perform in order to be "worthy".

2. A total absence of love; neglected and isolated. Sometimes this can occur when one child is loved and cared for and the other is not.

3. Being subjected to regular destructive criticism without any self esteem building or sense of approval.

4. Never being encouraged, noticed or "seen".

5. Being loved but it was never expressed; the child didn't know.

6. Poor examples of how to have a loving, caring, stable relationship that is safe. Witnessing the opposite: destructive, abusive, unpredictable, without love.

7. Being physically abused, perhaps with violence.

8. Being sexually abused and feeling like there was nowhere to turn.

9. Not having a healthy attachment to any adult with some predictability.

10. Poor authoritarian role models in key areas displaying bully behavior: modeling.

Five things we learn:

1. In order to carry out healthy adult relationships, one must have a healthy sense of self worth and self esteem.

2. Most people will realize their shortcomings of lower self worth and lower self esteem and take responsibility for this; or at least they have the ability to exercise humbleness which is needed in healthy inter-personal relationships.

3. For the bully, they have suppressed their hurt and damage, probably at a young age, in order to cope.

4. The suppression has caused a lack of the ability to "feel" in their adult life.

5. When a person cannot "feel", they are unable to empathize and "put themselves in your shoes". They are incapable. This is why you cannot rationalize with a bully.

What happens to the bully?

1. The bully actually experiences a sense of satisfaction when hurting others, not remorse.

2. This sense of satisfaction is perceived as being "in control" over another and therefore a false sense of power is created for the bully.

3. The power and self worth they feel they have lost is replaced by the delusion that power over someone will result in more worthiness for the bully.

4. The bully is threatened by smart, competent, kind people; they fear them, so they control by attempting to take their power away.

4. Understanding What Motivates a Bully

Understanding why a person engages in bullying behavior can help you better deal with him or her. For instance, when you recognize that the bully is insecure and unhappy instead of evil, maybe you won't feel so intimidated and wronged. And understanding what the bully gets out of his behavior can help you control your responses more effectively.

So, why is the bully a bully?

The bully's disrespectful behavior stems from a deep insecurity and a sense of low self worth that they have about themselves. Their bullying behavior says more about them than it does about you. The bully sees the target as more powerful, and perceives the target as a threat. Therefore the bully attempts to take control of the target.

Bullies act the way they do in order to get their needs met, in the only way they know how.

1. The bully feels threatened by the target's success.

2. The threat is a delusion – the bully feels a lower sense of self worth when he is around someone he perceives as more powerful.

3. This delusion (deep irrational belief) triggers anxiety. The bully feels the target's self assurance will expose his low self-confidence.

4. The bully's anxiety is only alleviated by inflicting suffering on others. Inflicting pain on others was probably learned by the bully early in life as a coping mechanism and maybe even rewarded in the workplace through promotion or not being held accountable for their behaviors. In order to gain back control, the bully deliberately targets the individual in order to gain power over them.

5. Interestingly, male bullies will use more overt, hostile forms of bullying such as overt verbal attacks, strong tone of voice and threats.

6. Female bullies will (generally) resort to more passive bullying approaches, such as manipulation, deviousness, vengefulness and exclusion.

7. These behaviors become obsessive to the bully, who is now "addicted" to the fix of having "power over" someone as opposed to facing their original lack of support from early on.

The bully only knows one way – power over. They have not experienced a shared sense of trust and power in their earlier relationships; they only know their way. In fact, it is like having a major interpersonal disability – the inability to share power with another.

Inflicting pain on others was probably learned by the bully early in life as a coping mechanism, and maybe even rewarded in the workplace through promotion or not being held accountable for their behaviors. The bully becomes addicted to this pattern.

How could a bully inflict such pain to a target and "live with him/herself" for doing so?

It is hard for us to understand how a person could treat another cruelly and yet not feel any remorse at all. Studies show that through a lack of self-awareness and childhood trauma of some kind, some people are unable to even recognize their own emotions, let alone others' emotions. Therefore the "normal" interpersonal expectations we have of one another – such as kindness, empathy, care and concern, inquisitiveness and general interest – are not met when interacting with a bully.

> The 'normal' interpersonal expectations we have of one another – kindness, empathy, care and concern, inquisitiveness and general interest – are not met when interacting with a bully.

Empathetic behaviors, such as calming fears, identifying with another's emotional state and being able to express care and concern, should not be expected from a bully. Bullies are incapable of feeling remorse and therefore they would not be inclined to show empathy.

The bully is afraid of not being in control. He is also afraid of being taken advantage of and appearing weak.

In a bully's past, to appear weak only brought on extreme pain; so the bully vowed to never be weak again. It wasn't safe. Through bullying others, the bully seems to "prove" to himself and others that he isn't weak or inferior. Bullying also gives a way to vent anger and pain – which is considerable. If others appear frightened or pathetic, the bully does not feel empathy but rather disgust. Why? Because the bully is repulsed and ashamed of his own feelings of weakness.

The bully does not worry about not getting along with others. Generally, most bullies do not possess the quality of self-reflection. The bully is so driven and desperate to fulfill his own wants and needs that other consequences of his actions don't even register with him.

Since the bully secretly feels inadequate and weak, any demonstration of fear or pain by a target only means one thing to him: "I am powerful. I am in control."

When the bully sees the fear and suffering created in another, he only sees his own mightiness. The bully doesn't notice that there is a real human being behind that anguish, feeling that pain. If the bully did notice, he wouldn't care. The bully is incapable – it's all about the bully.

Does a bully ever have feelings of discomfort about the pain caused to a target?

Sometimes – but if the bully does, she will quickly rationalize her behavior, convincing herself that the target somehow is to blame and that the target deserves it.

The bully cannot handle the emotional pain of another. The bully is so distraught about her own pain – she is self-absorbed.

Humans all want the same thing in life: to feel accepted, understood, loved and respected. Bullies want the same thing, too. (I know—they have a pretty harsh way of showing it!) But they do want the same things that you do – they just aren't as good at getting them as you are.

You might be thinking, "Well, I feel a little insecure myself and I don't go around beating people up." No, you don't. So, what *do* you do? Do you try to keep the peace, to avoid confrontation? Do you bend over backwards trying to please others, so they'll like you? Do you go overboard helping others, to feel needed? Do you usually maintain a "benefit of the doubt" approach and look for the best? Whatever you do – and whether it works or not – it's the best way you know how to get what you need in life. You are doing the best you can, with what you know so far in life. We are *all* doing the best we can. Every one of us, always.

> **Whenever I feel injured by someone else's actions toward me, I remind myself, "We are all doing the best we can."**

Whenever I feel injured by someone else's actions toward me, I remind myself, "They are doing the best they can." That doesn't mean I accept the behavior. I don't. But it helps me understand that her behavior is about her, not me. And, since I try not to take it so personally, I can respond much more constructively. Maybe from my response, she will understand that she can't get away with acting in the same way again. Or possibly she hadn't known how her behavior was affecting me and now she does. In either case, next time "the best she can" may just be a little better! I also remind myself of this when I'm disappointed or frustrated with my own actions. Instead of kicking myself, I try to see

32

how I can do better next time. Forgive the bully, forgive yourself—but take corrective action!

P.S. Did I always know this? No. Do I always do this? No – but I try. Becoming knowledgable is the key to empowerment. Confidence secures it. Keep going!

Experts generally agree that bullying behavior is developed in childhood and continues into adulthood if not corrected. A lot more could be said about the origins of bully behavior but I think it would be more helpful for you – you, who are on the receiving end of bullying – to focus on the behavior itself. Otherwise, you might get caught in the trap of over-sympathizing with or overanalyzing the bully, rather than protecting yourself from the behavior. Regardless of their inner motivations, bullies continue to bully because they continue to get away with it. Certain people present themselves as attractive targets for bullying. And, in many organizations, there simply isn't any penalty for bullying behavior.

5. Envy: The Main Drive Behind the Bully

Envy is one of the seven deadly sins and perhaps the most destructive. It is also the most secretive as people do not readily confess the fact that they may wrestle with envy, let alone openly discuss it with others.

Wikipedia states that **Envy** is an emotion that "occurs when a person lacks another's superior quality, achievement, or possession and either desires it or wishes that the other lacked it."

It can also derive from a sense of low self-esteem that results from an upward social comparison threatening a person's self image: another person has something that the envier considers to be important to have.

When the bully is faced with the realization that powerful people are around them – people who are confident, smart, socially acceptable, nice, kind, trustworthy and so on - the bully automatically feels her own lack in these areas and resorts to envy. She believes the target has "more", and she is unable to handle this "perceived" imbalance. The bully hates those who trigger the feeling of her own inferiority.

> "Those who are most distrustful of themselves are the most envious of others. Those who are the most weak and cowardly are the most revengeful."
> – William Hazlitt

Envy asks one thing: "Why not me? Why am I not smart, socially accepted, seen as kind, etc.?" When the bully feels inferior and that she cannot level things up, then she resorts to leveling things down. People with healthy self-images allow others the freedom to experience good fortune, while bullies are incapable of honoring someone else's successes; in fact they seek to destroy them. They are intent on the destruction of the happiness of others.

Once the bully experiences these intense feelings of envy, she quickly moves onto the thoughts of "Why not me?" and then seeks to destroy anyone that has more than her. The destruction phase becomes the addiction and the "fix" the bully needs in order to feel powerful once again. Highlighting the target as unworthy and undeserving is part of the bully's defense.

What you must know in order to handle envy:
1. Understand envy. It is what drives most bullying behavior.
2. Know that the roots of envy are borne out of the bully's low self-worth, not on your un-deservingness.
3. Recognize and even expect the bully's attacks; rather than being surprised, be prepared.

6. Types of Bullies

The majority of workplace bullying occurs with one's direct boss. Your boss has legitimate power over you, a subordinate. An insecure bully boss will seek to misuse this power in order to satisfy their own feelings of low self worth, instead of using their power to manage, guide and lead employees, and create a healthy productive work environment.

There is also what we call lateral bullying or peer to peer bullying, in which one peer bullies another. Many managers will often tell two co-workers to "work it out" or "go for a coffee and talk". Note: This can work if it is a simple conflict where both parties are interested in working out the details. This approach doesn't work when it is a case of workplace bullying because it is impossible to hold a peer accountable if there is no interest on the part of the bully. Authoritative power and support is needed for the target in order to truly correct the behavior.

There are five types of bullies:

A: Arrogant Bullies
B: Manipulative Bullies
C: Dictator Bullies
D: Victim Bullies
E: Suspicious Bullies

A: Arrogant Bullies

What they look like:

1. They are pre-occupied with themselves and their achievements;

2. They believe with full confidence that others should admire them and show deep respect towards them;

3. They take selfish unfair advantage of others without any guilt or regret;

4. They lack empathy and compassion for others.

What's going on inside:

1. They wrestle with "delicate" self esteem;

2. They are void of true love;

3. They feel their pretentious dreams about themselves are justifiable (to fill their emptiness).

The confusion:

1. They are often charismatic, fooling management that they can "lead" others.

2. They can be seen as "serving others" by buying lunch, etc., but only to serve their own needs as there is no consistency.

3. They over-shoot risk taking (which may look like a go-getter employee) but they will misuse resources and people for their own gain.

What can you do to cope?

1. Do not criticize them; they will crush you with no regard for your feelings.
2. Do show your admiration for them.
3. Do not compete with them.

B: Manipulative Bullies

What they look like:

1. They do not sincerely display guilt, remorse, regret or empathy. However, they will display these emotions with convincing confidence in order to get what they want.
2. Their overly charismatic persuasion is used to convince others that they are much more truthful, capable and trustworthy than they really are.
3. They do not have caring, trusting, open and vulnerable relationships as they lack a social conscience where "looking out for your neighbor" is present. Getting away with something, even at the expense of others, is a thrill.

What's going on inside:

1. They feel justified to be treated as exceptionally "special"; rules, laws, policies and collaboration do not apply to their psyche.
2. They have felt "wronged" in the past and therefore have

developed a sense of entitlement that the world owes them, so they can do whatever they want.

3. They may have been abused at a young age, and as a result stopped surfacing any feelings to avoid further pain. This abrupt halt to experiencing their own true feelings holds them back from their ability to sense and experience others' pain.

The confusion:

1. They display socially acceptable behaviors such as charisma, charm, fun, laughter and even warmth in order to draw you to trust them. The reason, however, is to gain your vulnerability and follower-ship. They will then play the game of manipulation, lying, cheating and deception in order to position you for their own gain.

2. Corporations reward these types of people, mistaking their aggressiveness for a drive for goal attainment and their extreme confidence and arrogance can be confused with capability and expertise.

3. They are skilled at moving in with their charm and creating a sense of trustworthiness in order to pit one co-worker against another, leaving people disjointed and uneasy with one another as opposed to united. This is where the bullies wants everyone, so no one will take them on.

What can you do to cope?

1. Be aware of overly captivating persuasiveness and do not let yourself be taken in by their overwhelming connect-ability and promises.

2. Stand united with others on your observations and insights, as attempting to survive this on your own will only create more confusion, hurt and loss of confidence for you.

3. Do not get caught fist fighting with them for power. They will always win, as they are not capable of caring about your feelings and concerns. Walk away; sooner rather than later.

C: Dictator Bullies

What they look like:

1. They "know better than you" and proceed to tell you so. They are unaware of other people's strengths and abilities, therefore they will not acknowledge your efforts and accomplishments.

2. They micro-manage. They expect your undivided attention to doing it "their way" and they expect you to obey their ideas and directives with unquestioning obedience.

3. They see the world as either black or white, in control or out of control. They will do everything to make sure it is in control, including controlling others.

What's going on inside:

1. They fear that their world will spin out of control if they do not "micro-manage" to harness control over all details.

2. They feel powerful and content only if in control. If someone else has an idea (power), they in fact feel threatened and take it as a massive insubordination that they will be seen as "less" because someone is offering "more".

3. Because of their fear of experiencing chaos, their need for control is greater than their value of honouring others' needs, building win-win relationships and working as a team.

The confusion:

1. One's natural tendency when controlled by another is to "push back". This will only get you in deeper, and dictator bullies will press in further. Standing up for yourself can serve to put you in a far worse position. Pick your fights.

2. They may appear confident at first, but as you know them better, you see that it is conceit.

3. You may feel that you "can help" by making a suggestion in a nice way when things are not running smoothly. This is the worst thing you could do: Controlling Bullies will see this as a massive threat to their self worth and proceed to "put you in your place". They will do anything to regain a position of being in control.

What can you do to cope?

1. Do not point out errors the bully made; be prepared for a fight.

2. Do not feel you can enlighten this person. Don't even think of it. They do not welcome anyone knowing anything more than they do.

3. Create an environment where they think they were the one to come up with an idea or suggestion.

D: *Victim Bullies*

What they look like:

1. They feel a lack of personal power and they are unable to share what they need. They are not assertive and instead resort to blaming others and making excuses for the fact that their needs are not met.

2. They reject what others want by being late or missing deadlines. They are negative, or whine when their needs are not met, instead of dealing with people in a more direct win-win way. They complain about their "bad luck" and not being appreciated enough.

3. They constantly believe that others are out to dominate and control them, so they drag their heels in making decisions, because they feel pushed. They will not very often admit mistakes or own a problem.

What's going on inside:

1. They look calm and easy going on the surface, but underneath is an unexpressed anger they do not know how to deal with or express. They are out of touch with their own needs and they are unable to express them with confidence and clarity.

2. They often ignore and protect themselves from others' requests, thinking they are gaining back a sense of control for themselves.

3. They are often jealous of others; they want the power others have, thinking they do not have the ability to claim any power for themselves. They come across as negative, often criticizing others and not taking responsibility for their actions. Making excuses and blaming others is easier.

The confusion:

1. They say one thing, yet have very different feelings inside. They are non-congruent and are out of alignment with their thoughts and feelings, leaving you puzzled many times.

2. They look relaxed and easy going, however, this is a front in order to appear in control. When you ask them to help out, or if a decision has been made, they hesitate and drag their feet, even though you may have communicated the urgency for getting something done.

3. Their negativity and blaming can be puzzling to those who genuinely want to connect and work with this person. It leaves others around them confused while trying to get things done.

What can you do to cope?

1. Do not count on them. Simply cover yourself with deadlines and commitments and do not expect them to comply with your requests. They will likely not follow through, even on the simplest of tasks. (Remember, it is not the task that is hard for them, it is the commitment to the task: they feel controlled in having to do anything on someone else's agenda or timing.)

2. They will often change, or not honor, what you thought to be a simple agreement between the two of you, leaving you frustrated when the deadline comes. Gather witnesses and document publicly, in order to gain support for your work completed.

3. Set clear expectations in all areas with solid documentation. Be clear that oppositional and negative displays of behavior are not tolerated and give specific examples of what this behavior is to you.

E: Suspicious Bullies

What they look like:

1. They tend to be hostile, sarcastic, secretive and argumentative: they do not trust others.

2. They seek others who are compliant and who will not threaten their decisions.

3. They read "hidden messages" that are not present in others as a "slight" to their character.

What's going on inside:

1. They have a very discouraging view of themselves, and they assume others have this same view of them as well. To protect their damaged confidence, they bury their self doubts and negative self images and substitute them with contempt and disregard for others; it is safer for them.

2. They do not give the benefit of the doubt when things are not as they seem; instead, they assume someone is "out to get them".

3. They blame others for their problems and do not take any responsibility for any wrongdoing. Others constantly "fail them".

The confusion:

1. They treat others with disregard and promote a lack of trust, when in fact they do not trust that others are not out to get them.

2. They are so worried and scared, yet the last thing they would do is reach out to another for help. Doing so would not feel safe, so they project to others that "it is not safe" to trust others, and act as if others were not trust-worthy.

3. They are so convincing that when they are being attacked by others they may begin to persuade you to question your own motives and actions. It is good to review your actions, but do not get caught in trying to please them.

What can you do to cope?

1. When this person questions you and perhaps attacks your motives, remember they are doing so for their own safety needs, not usually because of your incompetence. Remain calm and supportive, do not get defensive; it will only make matters worse.

2. Give as much information as you can, well in advance of any meetings, and allow for them to make choices. Choice is power.

3. If you have to deliver bad news to someone who is a suspicious bully, be prepared for a blow up; remember, he is only trying to protect his paranoia.

There are many types of bullies. Being truly aware of what you are dealing with is your first step to true empowerment. Avoid the confusion by becoming not only aware, but by internalizing the knowledge.

7. How Serious Is Bullying?

As we will discuss in Chapter 8, **Handling the Bully**, the levels of the bullying can range from minor to moderate to severe. Minor bullying might be a mere annoyance, such as the bully delighting in contradicting and making fun of the target in front of others. Moderate-level bullying escalates the harassment, causing the target considerable stress and possibly including name calling, heckling, sabotage, spreading rumours, lying to and about the target, and so forth. Severe bullying is extreme and dangerous. Subjecting the target to the tactics I have so far described for a sustained period of time can bring extreme strain to bear on the target's health, stress level, ability to perform their work and just to function. The bully might further intensify his bullying with threats, sabotage intended to do serious harm to the target's person or property, or physical aggression.

Is it possible for a bully to learn to become more aware of others' feelings? Certainly, but I wouldn't count on it. Remember, the bully's focus is riveted on her own unmet needs: to be accepted, to feel she is a person of worth, to feel in control, and so forth. This fixation keeps her attention on herself and prevents her from broadening her view to include others. And, since her aggressive, destructive behavior is not likely to get her the acceptance and respect she so desperately wants, the cycle may go on indefinitely. If, by chance, the bully gets uncomfortable twinges of guilt about abusing the target, she often will rationalize her behavior, convincing herself that the target somehow is to blame, that the target deserves it.

8. The Facts You Need to Know About Workplace Bullying

It is a well-known fact that 1 out of 6 people are bullied at work.

Of those being bullied, 25% will suffer greatly.

Did you know that 67% of those being bullied have the intention of:

1. Leaving their job (30%), or

2. Staying in their job and doing nothing (37%)?

Furthermore...

1. Those who said they discussed it with co-workers (47%).

2. Those who said they discussed it with friends and family (38%).

3. Those who confronted the bully (34%).

In addition:

1. Only 11% went to their manager.

2. Less than 8% went through the company's grievance procedure.

Where does this leave us?

We must remember:

1. Bullying is everyone's responsibility.

2. One out of four people will need our support: we must become aware of what to do in situations that involve bullying.

3. Consider a company of 600 people: 100 people may be bullied to some degree.

Also note:

1. When employees were asked if their workplace situation affects their family and primary relationships, 87% said yes.

2. Being bullied has a multiplication affect.

We all need to become informed about stopping workplace bullying. If you or anyone you know is struggling with being bullied at work, or perhaps you were bullied at work but you are still traumatized by the situation you went through...

Give the gift to yourself to get educated...

And remember, if it has not happened to you, it will happen to a close friend or colleague in your lifetime.

9. Behavior That Gets Rewarded Gets Repeated

So, let's turn to what specifically motivates bullying behavior. *What does the bully actually get out of it?* The age-old rule of motivation says "Behavior that gets rewarded gets repeated." Taking this further then, behavior that *doesn't* get rewarded will eventually extinguish itself, and behavior that is *punished (penalized)* should stop. Therefore the first step is to identify how you are "rewarding" the bully with your response, then changing your response to a non-reward or even a disincentive.

> Why People Bully:
> - To get what they want
> - To feel better (more powerful) about themselves
> - To release anger
>
> The first step to take is to identify how you're "rewarding" the bully with your response, then change the response to a non-reward, or even a disincentive.

The bully is trying to get his own way or humiliate someone so he can feel better about himself. Through bullying, he can also release anger. Sometimes the target might pose a particular threat to the bully, at least in the bully's eyes. So by "protecting his territory" the bully can maintain his power by keeping things the way they are. By squashing the target, the bully gets to feel victorious and powerful.

The intent of the bully is to embarrass and humiliate the target – to make her feel poorly about herself. Perversely, the bully can be very sensitive to how the target feels and therefore can cruelly manipulate the target's emotions. For instance, the target may start off feeling a bit insecure, perhaps as a part of his evolving personality, or possibly due to circumstances, such as being new to the organization, department or job. Being called a "wimp" by the bully further exacerbates the insecurity. Once the bully knows he has hit the "bull's eye", he continues his tormenting.

10. Common Bullying Tactics

A bully will use many different tactics, depending on the particular vulnerabilities he perceives in his targets. (For the different "types" of targets, please see **Who Do Bullies Target?** in Chapter 3.)

Here are some of the most common tactics workplace bullies will use:

1. Verbal abuse

2. Exclusion

3. Unfairness (crazy-making)

4. Lack of clarity

Bullying Tactic: Verbal Abuse

Verbal abuse occurs when hurtful words that attack or injure, are used at the expense of a target, and cause the target to believe a false sense of self.

The bully preys on the target's good nature of kindness and a forgiving attitude in order for the target not to challenge anything being said, but rather remain silent and confused. Silence and confusion are big wins for a bully.

Verbal abuse is hostile aggression where the impact on the target is hurtful. It comes in all forms, including name calling, putting down, criticizing, intimidation and a disrespectful tone of voice. In addition, the abuser rarely admits or recognizes his behavior, resulting in confusion and despair for the target.

Verbal abuse is a bullying tactic where the abuser is not interested in your answers or responses, even though he has questioned you or opened up a dialogue.

Why they say what they say:

1. They need to show power over the target in order to control the target.

2. They want to evoke an emotional response in the target in order to demonstrate their control and power.

Types of verbal abusers:

1. **Unaware:** "It's because I have to show her she is wrong again." This form of excuse is an opinion, not a truth. There is no room for curiosity or dialogue.

2. **Denial:** These people are not able to see, or refuse to see, that there are other win-win ways of communicating.

3. **Intentional:** This is usually as a result of a psychological problem, or an unresolved emotional problem, where the bully acts out in order to deliberately regain a sense of power from others (remember - bullying is intentional).

How do we typically respond?

1. **We push back:** We use negative communication such as verbal attacks, walk away before agreeing, announce an end a conversation, ignore the other person, or do not answer directly.

2. **We grovel:** This occurs when we are over-kind, even though we do not feel this way. We use emotional appeals to try to curb the abuse.

3. **We reason:** We try and make sense of the conversation with logic, statistics, and factual evidence in order to gain a win-win resolve.

Please note:

- These methods do not work with classic verbal abusers.

- Not all verbal abuse is bullying - however, that does not mean that there is not emotional damage.

- Whether the verbal abuser is aware or not, the behavior is still harmful.

- The three coping mechanisms often used, i.e., pushing back, groveling and reasoning, actually assist verbal abusers by giving them the upper hand.

How to best respond to verbal abuse:

1. Being aware if you are in a verbal abuse situation is key; in order to not expect a mature exchange of conversation.

2. Once you are aware, you can protect yourself emotionally by realizing this has nothing to do with you, but rather the verbal abuser's need to gain control.

3. Do not engage. Separate yourself emotionally and physically, and even say "This is not a good time for me to talk right now. I'd be happy to talk later when we can both converse."

Verbal abuse tactics that you should be aware of in terms of workplace bullying:

1. Spreading spiteful rumors; gossip and backstabbing.

2. False accusations about your performance and personhood.

3. Use of foul, offensive language.

4. Sarcastic humor with intent to harm.

5. Improper comments about your age, gender, religion, sex, race, color, past, opinions and beliefs.

6. Talking about the target in the third person when the target is present.

7. Threats or ultimatums.

8. Guilt or intimidation in order to control.

9. Being yelled at; alone or in front of others.

10. Deliberately minimizing and devaluing one's performance with refusal to acknowledge results.

11. Blaming – finding fault with the target and constantly highlighting the fault(s).

12. Placating, where the bully appears to be agreeing with a situation of why something has not occurred, but makes by a sarcastic statement that highlights the bully as "not being in the wrong" technically. The tone in which it is said leaves the target feeling as if they owe something to the bully. "I know we need to have sales meetings every Monday at 8:00 am and I really don't mind coming in early for these meetings. I mean, fighting traffic is what I do for a living!"

The key to responding to these types of bullying verbal abuse behaviors is:

1. When you hear a statement such as the above, ask yourself if there is any truth in the statement.

2. If there is truth, say sorry and move on.

3. If there is no or little truth, then let these statements go. Do not respond, do not argue, do not open any dialogue.

When bullies use verbal abuse in order to target and control another, they often do so in a way where their tone of voice is patronizing, disrespectful and hurtful. Bullies are also masters at throwing out accusations without proof, or using implying statements that cause the target to be seen in a less than attractive light. Anyone using these forms of verbal abuse must be held accountable by the target, co-workers and the organization in order for the bullying to stop.

Bullying Tactic: Exclusion

Exclusion occurs when a bully intentionally withholds or does not invite the target to meetings, discussions or group endeavors for the sole purpose of controlling the target by leaving them out. Information and connection are power. The bully seeks to destroy any attempt the target may have for power in order to maintain "control over" the target.

Exclusion tactics that you should be aware of in terms of workplace bullying:

1. Exclusion from meetings – not being told when or where the meeting will be held, or not being informed as to how to prepare, thereby leaving you looking unprepared.

2. Not speaking directly with you and resorting to email, texts, or other people to carry the message to you.

3. Withholding important information you need in order to do your job, or giving it to you at the last minute.

4. Refusing to delegate or assign work, then reprimanding you for not completing this work.

5. Withholding empathy or support when needed for problems faced, such as work challenges, or personal difficulties such as illness or a death in the family.

6. Not giving you support and attention, yet giving others support and attention.

7. Cutting off communication – a refusal to interact in any way.

8. Ignoring requests, emails, suggestions and opinions as if they were not even voiced.

9. Not inviting you to social gatherings, such as going for lunch, and then denying you were not invited.

10. Not being included in general conversation – no eye contact, snubbing, ignoring.

Exclusion is a subtle way to hold control over a target. Very often others are unaware of the bully's tactics, as the bully positions himself as innocent, with the target looking unprepared or not wanted. The target is often left alone to suffer.

Bullying Tactic: Unfairness or "Crazy-Making"

Unfairness is a broad term, and this normally occurs when usual procedures and conduct are expected, but are changed for the target. The target is left confused and bewildered, and feels a need to try harder. This is the "hidden agenda" or "can't win" double-bind conversation where you're stuck if you do, and stuck if you don't. The cycle is called "crazy-making" as there will never be a satisfactory completion.

"Crazy-making" is a term used where the bully uses their power-over in order to confuse, and keeps the target powerless by not adhering to fair practices, policies and conduct, although implying otherwise.

Here's how it works:

1. The bully accuses you of a behavior that she believes you should change.

2. You apologize, try to make amends, show concern in order to resolve. You enter into the dissatisfaction with curiosity.

3. As soon as you do, the bully changes tactics with a new problem, or minimizes your efforts to make amends.

Here's how you feel:

Confused: You are trying to connect and resolve.
Frustrated: You do not know what else to do; you can't seem to connect.

Remember:

The bully creates "crazy-making" in order to gain the upper hand and decrease your power. When you are confused and doubting yourself, you feel powerless.

What you can do:

1. Quickly identify and name this behavior as "crazy-making" and distance yourself from trying to resolve with the bully – it is a no-win situation.

2. What you can say: "This is crazy-making – there is no room to resolve this in a win-win way."

P.S. Having a short, clear statement that shows you are setting your boundary between you and the bully gives you back your control and power. The benefit is that you will not waste your time in confusion, wondering, and powerlessness. This is how to become Bully Free At Work™!

Unfair practices or "crazy-making" tactics that you should be aware of in terms of workplace bullying:

1. A demotion without cause.

2. Increasing responsibilities or workload without granting authority to complete the demands.

3. Repeatedly giving work at the last minute and expecting proper completion and perfection. Creating unreasonable demands, leaving the target to scramble.

4. Removal of job status or importance in an underhanded way without proper explanation.

5. Being reprimanded for a behavior, such as being late for a meeting, while other co-workers are not reprimanded for the same behavior.

6. Continual performance reviews with vague comments of unsatisfactory work without specific recommendations or documentation.

7. Not acknowledging an excellent contribution, while acknowledging others' contributions.

8. Many complaints about you without any factual backup. General accusations that you have no idea how to address.

9. Being given non-work related tasks to do, which holds you back from completing needed work; then being reprimanded or pressured to do needed work.

10. Continually taking the credit when things go well, but blaming you when things go wrong.

Bullying Tactic: Lack of Clarity

A bully's lack of clarity or vague responses leaves a target guessing, and thus unprepared and not in control. By not being clear, the bully takes away a target's power, leaving them scrambling for the truth. It is a tactic that promotes confusion, rather than empowerment or shared power.

Lack of clarity – how it happens:

1. Refusal to clarify job description and work expectations.

2. Changing expectations without notice or buy-in.

3. Setting tasks without timelines, then reprimanding for missing deadlines.

4. Changing one's mind constantly about expectations.

5. Giving vague directives in terms of technical or safety situations in order to set up failure.

6. Reversal of decisions previously agreed upon with little warning or proper explanation as to why.

7. Malicious deception, lying or cheating.

8. Demanding work be redone without explanation.

9. Purposefully sabotaging work performance or impeding completion of duties.

10. Complaining about a target, but not documenting specifically in order for the target to improve.

Lack of clarity leaves the bully with all the power, and the target confused.

A demanding boss who puts a lot of pressure on an employee may or may not be a bully. The work itself might bring stress, especially in situations with tight deadlines, a need for precision, no room for error, compensation tied directly to output, a sense of competition among workers, and confusing or conflicting procedures.

You can clarify whether your boss or work situation rises to the level of bullying by considering the criteria for bullying once again. To ascertain if you are being bullied, review these four bullying tactics once again and ask if you are experiencing these behaviors. Next, determine if you feel a level of disrespect with regard to experiencing your selected behaviors. Then ask if they are repeated frequently. If so, then seek to determine if these behaviors are intentional.

CHAPTER 3

Why Me?

> **Overview**
>
> 1. Who Do Bullies Target?
> 2. Are You Vulnerable to Bullying?
>   *Self-Test: Are You Wearing a Bull's Eye on Your Back?*
> 3. The Bullying Cycle
> 4. Steps an Organization Can Take to Be Bully Free At Work ™ and to Create a Respectful Workplace

I've named this chapter **Why Me?** because that is so often the question that targets ask themselves over and over again. Naturally, you want to understand why a person would pick you out of a crowd and then make your life miserable. But be cautious: asking why for too long can get you mired in doubts and insecurities about yourself and prevent you from moving toward actually solving the problem.

Why would anyone be bullied at all?

Ironically, bullies target people that they want to be like. The bully wants what the target has. The bully is jealous of the target. Because of this, the bully deliberately tries to take the target's power away. This is gratifying to the bully and they create a false sense of security for themselves by having "power over" someone.

People are bullied because people, co-workers, bosses and organizations allow this behavior to occur.

When you consider why you're being bullied, keep in mind two important points. First, bullying behavior is about the bully. She is going to bully *someone*, whether it's you or somebody else. She is the one with the problem. It's not about what you're doing wrong or whether or not you deserve it (you don't). Second, she picked you because you fit the bill in some way.

> **Bullying behavior is about the bully. She is the one with the problem.**

Maybe you're an easy target, so she can act out her aggressions and not suffer unpleasant consequences. Also, maybe there is something about you that threatens the bully. This can be a practical matter, such as her perceiving you as encroaching on her territory in some way. Or maybe you possess a trait which she lacks, such as being well liked and respected by co-workers, so you're a symbol of her failure. Still again, there might be a vulnerability about you that she sees in herself as a weakness, so she lashes out against it. Understanding why you were picked as a target might help you stop the bullying.

1. Who Do Bullies Target?

There is no conclusive evidence that you are more or less likely to be targeted by a bully based on your gender, age, ethnicity or any other demographic factor. It's based more on personal characteristics and circumstances.

> **The Top Reasons a Bully Will Target You:**
> 1. You are effective and capable in your job.
> 2. You are well liked and accepted by others.
> 3. You have integrity and high moral standards.
> 4. You are kind and capable of showing empathy to others.
> 5. You have a high tolerance level for difficult people.

Natural Targets

Bully targets are often "nice" people - friendly, approachable, trusting, more interested in cooperating than competing, obliging, patient and tolerant, sympathetic, forgiving and kind. The bully doesn't believe in the sincerity of the target's kindness, or if he does, he sees it as weakness. Because these people are approachable, trusting, and tolerant, they are easy prey for both the confrontational and manipulative behaviors of the bully. Bullies think they can get away with more from people who are tolerant and forgiving. And the bully is right. They're easy pickings...if the target does not know how to protect himself.

Honest and "nice" people have kindness as their primary value. Often they do not fully comprehend the interpersonal political goings-on in an organization. In fact, often they don't even know anything is going on at all! For this reason, they can be naïve about "how things really work" and they don't take steps to protect themselves. The bully exploits this innocence. Even when the target does catch on and realizes that the bully's behavior is out of line, he will fight back only with honourable responses, which don't stand a chance against the bully's dirty tactics.

Un-Empowered Targets

People who appear vulnerable to the bully are attractive targets. Some of the "nice" people I described above are seen as vulnerable by the bully, especially if they are lacking in assertiveness and self-esteem. The more the target is lacking in assertiveness and self-esteem, the more the target is vulnerable, or un-empowered. These people are overly trusting, non-confrontational, non-assertive, have low-esteem, a poor self-image, have a strong need for others to be happy, and sometimes feel pushed around and taken advantage of. Somewhere, early in life, they made up their minds as to what a good person is like. They behave like that and expect others to do so, too.

We humans have the tendency to assume that others share our values and motivations. Honest people assume others are honest; devious people assume others are devious; jealous people assume others are jealous, and so forth. Our values are the building blocks of who we are so we tend to think others are made of the same material. Because of their childlike trust in others, un-empowered people don't question others' motives when they should. Rather than approach interactions with a healthy open-mindedness as to the other person's intentions and values, they swallow whatever they are handed, hook, line and sinker. They are seeing and hearing everything through the filters of their own view of the world, and when things don't turn out the way they had expected, they're surprised and hurt. They might have the same sort of experience again and again, all the while building up hurt and resentment, but are not comfortable confronting the issue.

By picking on these vulnerable targets who won't fight back, the bully – who feels weak and vulnerable herself – is proving to herself and others that she is not weak.

"Different" Targets

Others who are different in some way from either the norm or from the bully are preyed upon. These differences might be physical or mental disabilities, physical or behavioral characteristics (stuttering, large nose, weight, etc.), sexual orientation, age, manner of dress, race, religion… the list could go on forever. The bully feels inadequate, alone, alienated, *different from,* others. So, by bullying these people, the bully is demonstrating that the target – not himself – is different, although he secretly believes he is the misfit.

Targets of Whom the Bully Is Jealous

People targeted by bullies are often successful, smart, good at their jobs and talented. They may have more education, a higher-ranked job, be paid more, or have more authority or influence than the bully. Socially, targets are often popular and well liked by others. They may be attractive and poised. They possess personal characteristics about which the bully feels particularly inadequate. In short, the bully is jealous.

Author Andrea Needham relates in her book, *Workplace Bullying*, that people with high emotional intelligence (sometimes referred to as having high EQs) are favorite targets of bullying. Emotional intelligence describes the capacity to understand one's own feelings; have empathy for the feelings of others; be less prone to fearfulness; and be socially poised, outgoing and cheerful. "Some individuals seem to fill a natural target role for the Workplace Bully. As research indicates…the Workplace Bully focuses on Targets who are competent and who have the ability to build and sustain good relationships." Davenport et al[10] points out that their sample of individuals who had been bullied were individuals who "Daniel Goleman would consider to be 'emotionally intelligent' (EI)."[11] (Daniel Goleman is the developer of the concept of Emotional Intelligence).

Targets Who Threaten the Bully's Control

A bully may also target people who threaten his territory, whether that threat is real or imagined. Maybe they don't go along with how the bully is doing things. Possibly they respectfully disagree with the bully or tactfully point out a mistake. Or perhaps they stand up to the bully directly. The target might have authority or influence in an area important to the bully, such as having been assigned a project that the bully wants. It may be the target's mere presence that is threatening, and the bully assumes that the target wants to take power away from him. In these cases, regardless of the target's actual intentions and ability to threaten the bully's territory, the trigger is the bully's fear of losing control.

---

10   Davenport et al, p. 70.
11   Needham, A.W. Workplace Bullying. Penguin Books, 2003, p. 35.

Situational Targets

Some bullying is situational. For instance, a bully will pounce on a new person in the department or organization. The newcomer, who is already a bit insecure in the new surroundings, eager to fit in, and hasn't yet established a social support system, can be a sitting duck.

According to the Workplace Bullying and Trauma Institute, "Bullies test the field, especially with new employees. They look for the targets who put up no resistance to attacks. Approximately 75% of the workforce do not tolerate being controlled by another person. The bully backs off when resisted. Behavioral researchers speak of an aggressor's mental calculation of her effort/benefit ratio. The people who require more effort to aggress against than is considered worth it to the aggressor are no longer seen as targets. That is, bullies are lazy. They want an easy mark." [12]

Some Characteristics of People Targeted by Bullies:

Natural Targets
"Nice" people - friendly, approachable, trusting, cooperative, obliging, patient, tolerant, sympathetic, forgiving and kind.

Un-Empowered Targets
"Over-nice" people (people who have all the above traits, but to extreme) - non-assertive, low self-esteem, poor self-image, avoid confrontation, need other people to be happy, often feel taken advantage of and pushed around.

---

[12] Workplace Bullying and Trauma Institute

"Different" Targets
People with differences (such as physical or mental disabilities, physical or behavioral characteristics), sexual orientation, age, manner of dress, race or religion.

Targets of Whom the Bully Is Jealous
Successful; smart; compentent; talented; well-educated; higher-ranked job, higher pay, or more authority or influence than the bully; popular and well liked; attractive; poised.

Targets Who Threaten the Bully's Control
Willing to disagree with the bully, tactfully point out mistakes, stand up to the bully directly, have authority or influence in the bully's "territory".

Situational Targets
Newcomers to a company or department, anyone in the "wrong place at the wrong time".

2. Are You Vulnerable to Bullying?

As we have discussed, bullies sometimes choose targets who they resent, who they are jealous of, who are "different", or who pose some sort of threat in the bully's eyes. Many of these reasons are situational (you got the job the bully wanted) or are inherent (you're better looking). Bullies also like to target vulnerable people, people who may lack in self-esteem and assertiveness. These targets are easier to abuse because they don't fight back.   Are you vulnerable? Un-empowered? Then you might be wearing a bull's eye on your back. Look at the following self-test to see whether you are especially vulnerable to bullying.

Self-Test: Are You Wearing a Bull's Eye on Your Back?

How vulnerable to a bully attack are you? Rate yourself on the following characteristics below to find out. Be as honest and objective as you can be.

Personality characteristics
(circle one number for each characteristic)

Timid: Do you tend to be timid; hate confrontations; strongly prefer safe, routine situations? Or are you more assertive, asking for what you want, sticking up for yourself when necessary, but still disliking confrontation? Or are you downright bold, aggressive at times, don't mind confrontations?

Timid		Assertive		Aggressive
5	4	3	2	1

Do you bend over backwards to accommodate others, even to a point of being a sucker sometimes? Are you cooperative, as long as you're sure the other party also wants a win-win? Or are you competitive, needing to win at any cost?

Rescuing		Cooperative		Competitive
5	4	3	2	1

Are you totally "up front," 100% truthful no matter what, and tend to expect others to be the same, often confused when they're not? Are you generally honest and direct, but take some care about the effects of what you're saying? Or are you shrewd, good at figuring out how to manoeuvre the best outcome for yourself?

Honest to a fault		Direct and open		Shrewd
5	4	3	2	1

Do you get really worked up when someone is treated unfairly, even if you don't particularly care for the person? Or are you more generally fair-minded, but still don't mind when people you like (or yourself) get an extra advantage? Or do you consider a good outcome to be one where you get what you want? Crusader of justice   Fair-minded   Self-serving 5   4   3   2   1
Are you a sucker, believing everything you're told by everyone? Do you, while maintaining an open mind, consider the motives of the person telling you something, as well as their knowledge of the matter? Or is your first reaction to almost everything suspicion, believing that people mainly say and do things for their own gain? Gullible   Open-minded   Cynical 5   4   3   2   1
Do you instantly "feel" the hurt when you see someone in pain, and be able to automatically put yourself in their shoes, sometimes feeling that you are carrying the burdens of the world? Do you try to be considerate of others' needs and feelings, but not to a point where it interferes with your life? Do you pride yourself for telling it like it is, although people who are "too sensitive" often take offence? Empathetic   Considerate   Insensitive 5   4   3   2   1
Do you tend to do anything to accommodate others, even if very inconvenient for you and you suspect it won't be appreciated? Are you happy to oblige someone, as long as it isn't a big inconvenience? Do you make sure you take care of "Number One," and not worry about whether others are satisfied? Over-obliging   Cooperative   Self-centered 5   4   3   2   1

Top reasons a target is bullied, based on their vulnerabilities:

1. The target has a challenge speaking up assertively for himself.

2. The target subscribes to "peace at any price" and may have trouble showing anger to serve as a boundary.

3. The target feels guilty saying no, thus might sacrifice himself to others.

4. The target has high needs approval where he turns to self-doubt if someone does not like him.

5. The target is over-responsible and over-gives in order to fit in, and puts others ahead of himself to keep the peace.

Most targets invite the bully to attack them at some level, due to a disbelief and inability to set assertive boundaries.

3. The Bullying Cycle

When you're the target of workplace bullying, the last thing in the world it feels like is that you have control over what is happening. And yet you do. When workplace bullying begins, a cycle starts. As soon as you become aware of what is going on, you can begin to break the cycle.

The bullying cycle occurs when:
1. First, the bully is triggered due to sensing someone has more of something – power, kindness, intelligence, etc. The bully is the one who starts the bullying cycle, regardless of what's happening in the workplace.

2. The bully chooses to act out by trying to have "power over" the target.

3. The bully's aim is for the target to submit, comply, be afraid, be embarrassed and to back down.

4. The target's first response is one of confusion as they look to find the best. They try to accommodate or appease the bully, in order to maintain peace and professionalism.

5. The bully re-offends.

The cycle begins because the bully gets what they want – the target does not challenge. The target may be caught off guard and so respond with a socially acceptable response (as many of us were trained as children to do), such as ignoring the insult or agreeing to the demand. Maybe the target is embarrassed, and lacks the immediate composure to respond in an assertive way. In many cases, the person being bullied will generously assume it happened because of one of *his* failings and will try to please the bully. The bully has won and is satisfied.

> In many cases, the person being bullied will generously assume it happened because of one of his failings and will try to please the bully.

But not for long. Soon, something triggers her again and there is another bullying episode. The target once again tries harder to ignore, pacify or accommodate the bully. In between separate bullying incidents, there is a gradual rising of tension and uncertainty in the air for the target, to which he continues to try to adapt to and cope. And so goes the cycle…

It is a fact that if you place a frog into hot water, it will immediately jump out and hop away. But if you place a frog into cold water and gradually heat the water, the frog will remain there, even though you bring the water to a boil, killing the frog. That's because the temperature change is gradual and the frog adapts to the temperature change without knowing the danger it is in.

As long as the target denies or minimizes the bullying behavior, he is encouraging it to continue. Breaking the cycle will happen only when the target acknowledges that he is being bullied; and when he realizes that this is about the bully, not himself, and that he, the target, is not to be blamed. As soon the target recognizes this and begins to stand up for himself and bully proof himself, he is no longer as desirable a target for many bullies. Remember, the bully feels weak and inadequate and so prefers to prey on the weak and defenceless.

> As long as the target denies or minimizes the bullying behavior, he is encouraging it to continue. Breaking the cycle will happen only when the target acknowledges that he is being bullied.

Who does the target turn to when they have experienced workplace bullying?

1. Targets try to reach out to co-workers and friends at work for support first, before attempting any other means of support.

2. Targets turn to Human Resources and their direct boss as a means of support nearly last in terms of overall support at work.

Many targets experience the lack of accountability and follow through with regard to holding workplace bullies accountable for their behavior. To approach one's boss can serve as more of a threat than a support. Therefore it is important to "bully proof" yourself in order to be as strong as you can be. In addition, if you're being adversely affected by your work situation, even if it isn't the result of bullying, you still need to safeguard your emotional, mental, physical well-being. Consider the methods and skills in Chapter 7, **Empower Yourself.**

How do peers and co-workers cope with witnessing workplace bullying?

In most companies without protection against workplace bullying behavior, these common situations arise with regard to peers and co-workers who witness bullying behavior toward another co-worker:

- Peers and co-workers tend not to see the true effects the target is experiencing, as the bully seeks to use their tactics toward the target on a more subtle one-to-one basis in order to avoid creating any support that may occur from co-workers.

- When co-workers and peers actually do witness the bullying behavior toward another, they tend to pull back in silence. They are fearful for themselves, and they weigh out the risk of supporting the target versus personally pulling back.

- The main reason they will not stand up for a target is because they feel they would not have any power to make things better.

- Interestingly, targets turn to co-workers and peers

for support, yet co-workers and peers often feel ill-equipped to help.

- Some co-workers and peers will resort to denial and avoidance in order to cope personally, leaving the target more isolated.

How does an organization typically react or cope with workplace bullying?

Most organizations without protection against workplace bullying behavior typically resort to these behaviors when a workplace bullying situation concern is voiced by a target:

1. The organization may tend to minimize the situation, putting the onus on the target to "try harder" and "not take things so personally."

2. The organization, not knowing how to deal with the situation as it is highly subjective, will often choose to ignore the requests for help by the target, which only serves to further reward the bully. The company tolerates the bully without direct communication of the problem.

It takes courage and confidence to address workplace bullying behavior. It also takes time, energy and resources up front in order to effectively deal with such situations. A lot of companies see navigating through such subjective opinions as a cost to overall productivity. An organization's greatest wish may be that people who are unable to cope with these challenges would go away. However, this is a short-term solution. In reality, workplace bullying severely affects 25% of the work force; and the long-term costs, direct and indirect, far outweigh the short-term expenses of addressing this disrespectful, demoralizing and disruptive behavior.

Workplace bullying behavior can blindside a perfectly normal, healthy and happy employee. In order for co-workers, bosses and the company to cope, and therefore not address the situation and support the target, these myths are often surfaced:

1. "You're just taking things too personally. That's just the way (that person) is."

2. "You're just emotional."

3. "It's just a personality clash."

4. "Weak and incompetent employees attract bullies; toughen up."

5. "Our company respects toughness."

Workplace bullying is none of the above. Workplace bullying is all about power over another, thereby weakening the target. If left unattended, the target, through trying to hang in there, eventually breaks – physically, mentally, emotionally and spiritually.

4. Steps an Organization Can Take to Be Bully Free At Work ™ and to Create a Respectful Workplace

1. Awareness and education about bullying behaviors is key. Knowledge is power.

2. Shared commitment to creating workplace bullying policies (what) and procedures (how) in order to hold employees accountable for negative workplace bullying behaviors.

3. Measurement and accountability - in performance reviews, and one-on-one conversations between boss and co-workers as well as peers. Dealing with negative workplace behaviors with Documentation that is taken seriously and conducted in a safe environment.

4. Rewards for those who assist and create respectful workplace behaviors.

Ultimately, creating a Bully Free Workplace is attractive for creating employee retention, attracting new employees and creating the needed synergy and team building, in order to solve high level problems and create maximum profitability and enjoyment of one's job.

> If you ignore improper behavior, it means you condone it.

In Chapter 5, **So What Can You Do? – First Steps**, I will discuss in detail what steps you can take to stop bullying behavior against you.

Chapter 4

Effects of Workplace Bullying

> **Overview**
>
> 1. Symptomatic Effects of Being Bullied
>   *Self Test: How Bullying Is Affecting You*
> 2. The Full Price of Bullying

1. Symptomatic Effects of Being Bullied

> Bullies basically lack the ability of self-reflection, so they never assess the fairness or kindness of their actions.

Being bullied is being emotionally stalked by a person who, for whatever reason, sees you as a threat and who will do pretty much anything they want to get rid of you. And, since she has no sense of fair play and has well-developed skills of deception and manipulation, you're pretty much dead center in her crosshairs.

Because adult bullying is so dark and cruel in its very nature, a person being bullied can begin to suffer ill consequences almost immediately. The target will experience physical, emotional, mental and behavioral symptoms.

Physical symptoms, caused largely by stress and sleep deprivation, can include headaches, muscle pain, increased heart rate, high blood pressure, breathing problems, digestive problems, a weakened immune system (susceptibility to illness) and hair loss, to name but a few.

Emotional problems can consist of depression, anxiety, mood swings, feelings of worthlessness and suicide.

Some of the mental symptoms targets may experience are the inability to concentrate, foggy thinking, obsession over the bullying, and negative thoughts about life.

According to Namie and Namie[13], founders of the Workplace Bullying and Trauma Institute, the top 12 health consequences for bullied targets are:

- Sleep disruption (84%)
- Loss of concentration (82%)
- Severe anxiety (94%)
- Feeling edgy (80%)
- Obsession over bully's motives and tactics (76%)
- Stress headaches (64%)
- Avoidance of feelings and/or places (49%)
- Shame or embarrassment causing a change in routine (49%)
- Racing heart rate (48%)
- Flashbacks (46%)
- New muscle or joint aches (43%)
- Diagnosed depression (41%).

---

13   Namie, G., Namie, R., The Bully at Work. Naperville, IL. Sourcebooks, Inc. 2000. p. 61.

Self-Test: How Bullying Is Affecting You

Do you know how bullying is affecting you? Look at the following table, which is an abbreviated list of the adverse effects of bullying, and place a checkmark next to the effects that you're experiencing.

How Bullying Is Affecting Me	Me (normally)	Me (being bullied)
Physical symptoms:		
Headaches	☐	☐
Sore muscles	☐	☐
Jitteriness	☐	☐
Nervousness	☐	☐
Gritting teeth (sore jaw)	☐	☐
Heartburn	☐	☐
Indigestion	☐	☐
Decreased/increased appetite	☐	☐
Light-headedness	☐	☐
Racing pulse	☐	☐
Increased blood pressure	☐	☐
Chest pain	☐	☐
Heart palpitations	☐	☐
Unable to get to sleep	☐	☐
Unable to stay asleep	☐	☐
Fatigue/exhaustion	☐	☐
Decreased sex drive	☐	☐
Weight gain/loss	☐	☐
Skin breakouts	☐	☐
Hair loss	☐	☐
Increased sweating	☐	☐
Nausea	☐	☐

How Bullying Is Affecting Me	Me (normally)	Me (being bullied)
Emotional symptoms:		
Depression	☐	☐
Anxiety	☐	☐
Feelings of dread	☐	☐
Fear	☐	☐
Panic attacks	☐	☐
Sadness	☐	☐
Moodiness	☐	☐
Anger	☐	☐
Numbness	☐	☐
Feelings of hopelessness	☐	☐
Guilt	☐	☐
Dread going to work	☐	☐
Don't care about anything	☐	☐
Feelings of shame	☐	☐
Feelings of worthlessness	☐	☐
Thoughts of suicide	☐	☐
Paranoia	☐	☐
Jitteriness	☐	☐
Tearfulness	☐	☐
Feeling like screaming	☐	☐
Mental symptoms:		
Confusion	☐	☐
Forgetfulness	☐	☐
Disorientation	☐	☐
Inability to concentrate	☐	☐
Difficulty making simple decisions	☐	☐
Nightmares	☐	☐

How Bullying Is Affecting Me	Me (normally)	Me (being bullied)
Obsession over bullying situation	☐	☐
Brain lockup (Unable to think)	☐	☐
Flashbacks	☐	☐
Negative thoughts	☐	☐
Behavioral symptoms:		
Isolating myself from others	☐	☐
Becoming dependent on others	☐	☐
Becoming withdrawn from friends and loved ones	☐	☐
Fighting with loved ones	☐	☐
Neglecting my appearance	☐	☐
Neglecting my health (diet, exercise, sleep)	☐	☐
Increased alcohol/drug use	☐	☐
Poor work performance	☐	☐
Neglect of financial matters	☐	☐
Neglect of pets	☐	☐
Increased smoking	☐	☐
Risky behavior	☐	☐
Obsessive behaviors	☐	☐
Increasing inability to go to or remain at work	☐	☐
Reliance on sleep aids and tranquilizers	☐	☐
Unable to motivate myself	☐	☐

All of these symptoms in turn take their toll on the target's everyday life, including their job, their family life, their social life and their financial matters. They can also start relying on and even abusing medications to help them sleep and to distract them from their pain.

2. The Full Price of Bullying

People who endure bullying can start to see their world crumbling around them. And just at the time when you most need clarity of mind and energy, you may feel utterly worn out, confused and at the end of your rope. Perhaps you've distanced yourself from those who you normally rely on for support, by isolating yourself and neglecting important relationships, or by fighting with loved ones.

And the price of bullying is higher still. It can take an enormous toll on your health, keep you awake at night, and send your stress level skyrocketing. Work performance almost certainly suffers, which can lead to more pressure in other areas of your life, including financial. Workplace bullying can also force you to make unwanted choices about your work. The trauma and strain of the bullying can put you under tremendous pressure to leave your job. But maybe you *like* your job and don't want to leave. Possibly due to your length of service, you have built up some nice benefits that you don't want to give up. Perhaps you're not in a financial position to make a move. Maybe you don't feel you would be able to get the same job at another company.

You may not be able to stop a bully attack from happening to you in the first place, but you can minimize its consequences. Recognizing the problem is the first step. Maybe you feel that you let it go on longer than you should have. Don't worry – better late than never! Start from where you are, empower yourself as we will discuss in later chapters, and you can emerge from this experience intact, even stronger than you were before.

The main reasons people "put up with" workplace bullying behavior are:

1. They didn't recognize the behavior as bullying. Key: gain awareness of all bullying behaviors.

2. Fear of rejection and loss of acceptance and harmony with another. The target is fearful of addressing the conflict. She perceives addressing the conflict as an unsafe unsettling situation, as opposed to a supportive, solution-based initiative. Key: Create a mechanism for setting a safe environment for having crucial conversations that count.

3. Fear of "not being heard" or supported at work. Key: Develop communication systems for people to feel safe to express their needs and concerns with regard to workplace bullying behavior.

4. A "forgiving spirit" in which the target lives in hope that the bully will change somehow.

Workplace bullying behavior is psychological as opposed to physical. It is difficult to detect, and there are currently very few workplace-bullying policies in most companies, and even fewer laws worldwide, to protect targets.

Most targets go through these steps when they are being bullied:

1. **Naivety** – "I expect the best from others."
2. **Self-doubt** – "What did I do to cause this?"
3. **Disbelief** – "I can't believe they're doing that."
4. **Denial** – "They must have had a bad childhood."
5. **Delusion** – "If I act this way, they'll change."
6. **Searching** – "What should I say or do to change this?"

Targets search for a win-win – it's the natural thing to do for most people when interpersonal conflict occurs. When the bully does not return the same concern to work out the problem, this sends the target into a pathway of self-doubt. This causes the target to lose self-confidence and feel a sense of powerlessness.

Remember: You cannot rationalize or negotiate with a bully. Bullies are incapable of empathy and caring and they avoid any form of inter-personal discussion.

Because negotiation is a shared form of respect, it goes against the bully's need for self-preservation to have "power over" another.

So what should a target's focus be in regard to interacting with a bully? To bully-proof themselves first.

It is important for the target to realize that being bullied says more about the bully than it does about them. There is <u>never</u> an excuse for disrespectful, deliberate and harmful behavior toward another.

> **Though you cannot go back and make a brand new start, my friend, you can start now, and make a brand new end.** — Unknown

CHAPTER 5

So What Can You Do? – First Steps

> ## Overview
>
> 1. Four-pronged Response to Bullying
>   *Assignment: Stating the Problem*
> 2. Protect Yourself
>   *Exercise: Casting Yourself Forward One Year*

The way you respond to the bully – whether you avoid her, confront her, try to work it out with her, report her, or even leave your job – will depend on the level of bullying, how it affects you, and your particular situation. Chapter 8, **Handling the Bully**, discusses in detail possible ways to respond to a bully based on three levels of bullying: minor, moderate and severe. In this chapter, I'd like to talk about steps you should take in order to take care of yourself physically, emotionally and mentally, and how to protect yourself in practical ways, regardless of the level of bullying or your particular situation.

1. Four-Pronged Response to Workplace Bullying

Your knee-jerk response might be fight or flight, but handling a bullying situation needs a four-step response:

1. **State the problem**
   - Acknowledge the bullying.
   - Know that the bullying is about the bully, not you.

- Understand how bullying affects you.

2. **Protect yourself**
   - Bully-proof yourself.
   - Document the bullying.
   - Protect your health.
   - Know that you will get through this.

3. **Empower yourself**
   - Increase your level of wellness.
   - Take care of your physical health.
   - Manage your stress level.
   - Nurture yourself.
   - Enlist support, have some fun, meditate.
   - Build your self-esteem.
   - Develop your strengths.
   - Increase your options.
   - Build decision-making skills.
   - Learn to assert yourself.

4. Take action

State the Problem

Stating the problem means acknowledging the bullying; understanding who has the problem (realizing that the behavior is about the bully not you); and understanding the effects of the problem on you.

Acknowledge the Bullying

It's really important to acknowledge the bullying - to actually name it. "I'm being bullied." You can't solve a problem until you define what the problem is. When you are first subjected to bullying, it's natural to not recognize it. A coworker is abrupt with you and – being the understanding person that you are – you write it off to a bad day. When it happens again, you attribute it to the stress he's under. Or you begin to doubt yourself, asking "What did I do to cause that behavior from this person?" At some point though, you need to begin to recognize it for what it is. Otherwise, you run the risk of putting up with the abuse, trying to figure it out, and to accommodate or even change the person's behavior. You'll speculate that "he must be insecure because..." or "he probably thinks that...". Before you know it, you're at your wits' end, the only comfort being that you can complain regularly about the bully over a cup of coffee to your best friend. The bully has become the villain, which makes you the victim. The powerless victim.

> **You can't solve a problem until you define what the problem is.**

The mere act of naming it immediately gives you perspective and distance and clears up a lot of confusion about what is going on and why, especially when bullying is subtle and devious. Because you're a kind, trusting person, your usual practice is to give the benefit of the doubt to people in situations. So, if someone makes a subtle "put down" and you haven't identified their behavior as bullying, you will feel confused. You'll question whether or not it was your imagination, wondering what you had done to provoke or deserve it, replaying the exchange over and over in your head. (And we all know how that exercise can sap one's emotional energy!). You may blame yourself for being too sensitive (another emotional hit) and at the same time be angry that you didn't stand up for yourself.

Then, there's the feeling of shame and hurt. Guilt is what you feel when you believe you made a mistake, but shame is what you feel when you believe you *are* the mistake, that you somehow deserve the treatment you're getting. Targets run a high risk of feeling shame.

> Guilt is what you feel when you believe you made a mistake.
>
> Shame is what you feel when you believe you are the mistake.

Unfortunately, although you may not take the other person to task for a disrespectful remark, your self-esteem has suffered several serious blows. On the other hand, if you have identified the person as a bully, you're quite clear about what happened: he made a remark to try to make you suffer. Why? Because he's a bully and that's what bullies do. You might still feel hurt and angry that it happened. You might even put your finger on the precise issue or event that triggered his bullying and thus know better how to fend off future attacks. But it's no longer about you; it's about the bully.

If you name it – that is, identify clearly for yourself that a particular person is bullying you – you'll be able to handle all kinds of situations more capably. Instead of falling for the deceptions and antics of the bully again and again, you will see the pattern and be able to take defensive action.

Not Naming It	Naming It
Confusion	Clarity
Absolute trust	Healthy scepticism
Naiveté	Ability to see patterns
Easily blindsided	On the alert
Effort to appease	Effort to avoid or prevent
Self doubts	Knowing whose problem it is
Guilt about being successful	Pride in being successful

Understand How Bullying Affects You

Bullying can have countless and potentially devastating effects on people - emotionally, physically, socially, functionally and financially. As we saw in Chapter 3, targets of bullying can suffer a long list of physical, emotional, mental and behavioral symptoms.

Targets often feel like weaklings about the way they are reacting to being bullied. Needless to say, they often report enormous relief when they realize they are not the only ones who suffer these effects. It is important to understand *and write down* how bullying is affecting you, for some obvious and some not-so-obvious reasons.

First, it will remind you that your experience of being bullied is a real problem. You will be less likely to minimize it. It will help you notice effects that otherwise you might shrug off. A target often begins to experience distorted judgment as bullying continues and, before long he begins to adapt to the situation. He gets used to tension headaches, a stiff neck and stomach aches. Not being able to sleep becomes par for the course, or sleep aids become the rule rather than the exception. He stops noticing that he isn't concentrating well. Getting it down on paper will also remind you that these things are happening and that they started happening *after* the bullying started. Your documentation will provide an undeniable and constant reality check.

> **It is important to understand and write down how bullying is affecting you.**

It will help you isolate bullying as the culprit and therefore maintain better control of other aspects of your life. Life can get confusing and stressful for a bully target. Problems outside of work (such as with your spouse or partner, or with friends) may develop. Small irritations may escalate into huge problems that threaten your relationships. Staying aware of how the bullying is affecting you may give you more insight into and control over your behavior with friends and family.

Acknowledging that you're being bullied and understanding its effects also enables you to convey more clearly with friends and family about what's going on. Using the term workplace bullying is important, so that what is happening is seen as a pattern of behavior, rather than isolated incidents, by those whom you may rely on for support and advice. Refer again to the checklist of symptoms in Chapter 4 to remind yourself of the effects the workplace bullying is having on you.

If it comes to discussing the problem with your supervisor, Human Resources, management, a counselor or a legal representative, you'll need to be clear about the ill effects that workplace bullying has been having on you. This will underline the severity of the problem. It will also keep the focus where it belongs, which is on the behavior and its effects (rather than on the bully).

Admit Your Anger

Admit that you are angry about what is being done to you. If you don't, your anger will go underground, and may manifest in depression, anxiety, addictions and a host of other reactions. You don't have to wallow in anger. But admitting your outrage over what is happening, rather than burying it where it will continue to fester, will help you move on.

Remind Yourself That It Is About the Bully

Of all the questions you might ask about bullying, the one you might be tempted to ponder the most is the one you should actually concern yourself with the least. That question is Why? Asking "Why am I being bullied?" can take you down the trail of worrying that you're unlikeable, questioning if you're a "good person", wondering whether you're being punished for personal failings, and so on. As I said in Chapter 3, **Why Me?**, you should try to remember that it is about the bully.

Okay then - why is she is a bully? You may have some insight as to why she resorts to bullying to get by in life. A certain amount of understanding can be beneficial. Seeing her as an unhappy human being rather than as an evil villain has the positive effect of releasing you from feeling like a helpless victim. Also, seeing that she is acting out from her own problems may help you avoid thinking there is something wrong with you. Don't spend too much time speculating about why she is the way she is, though. And don't get in the habit of complaining about her to other co-workers. It's not constructive, it's disrespectful, and it will only add fuel to the fire. Your focus should be not on her, but on her unwanted behavior.

Assignment: Stating the Problem

If you recall from Chapter 1, the definition of bullying has two main parts, the action (repeated, deliberate, disrespectful behavior) and the effect (harm to the target). At this point, you have a pretty good idea about whether or not you are being bullied (see Self-test, Are you being bullied? in Chapter 2) and you understand how it is harming you (see Self-test, How bullying is affecting me, in Chapter 4). Now it's time to put your statement of the problem in writing.

You'll need a blank journal or notebook for the following assignment and for other entries and assignments as you work through the processes in this book.

- On a blank page in your journal, write "Statement of Problem" at the top. Then describe the parts of the problem:
  - **Who** is doing the bullying?
  - **What** does the behavior consist of?
  - **How often** does the bullying occur? Can you show that it is repeated?
  - **What are the effects** of the bullying on you? Your statement should be short, possibly one to three sentences. It is not necessary to add details.

- Stating the problem is the first step in deciding how to handle it. Later in this book, you will identify your options, evaluate them and, finally, decide what you want to do. For now, though, I'll just ask you to create headings for the other decision-making steps, and leave the pages blank.

- Below your statement of the problem, write the following headings for the next three pages:
  1. "Options" - Leave the rest of the page blank for now.
  2. "Evaluate Options", next line: "Pros:" and "Cons".
  3. "Choose an Option" - Identify actions to address obstacles.

Example: Statement of problem

Who: Paul Harwood

What/How Often: Makes fun of me in front of others by pre-calling poor job performance on my part; not giving me specific deadlines and then saying I was late turning in my project. Each time I've been in contact this past week, an incident such as above has occurred.

The Effects: This is causing me insomnia; and it is hard to concentrate on my job. I also feel left out and demoralized, and am beginning to doubt my own abilities.

Step #1:   Options (leave rest of page blank)

Step #2:   Evaluate Options
            Pros: Cons:
            (leave rest of page blank)

Step #3:   Choose Option - Identify action steps to address any obstacles.

            (leave rest of page blank)

2. Protect Yourself

There are several basic steps you can take to protect yourself from workplace bullying. You can become a less obvious, tempting target. You can also keep a record of the workplace bullying that not only helps you to maintain a perspective about what is happening, but could prove useful later if you decide to report the bullying. Above all, protect your health. And know that you will get through this.

Bully-Proof Yourself

Naturally, it's best to prevent the workplace bullying as early in the game as possible. Before it begins is best! But how? By reducing or eliminating the "rewards" that the person experiences when he bullies you. Examine the Bully Target profile in Chapter 3, **Why Me?** for insight about why you may be a target. What behaviors are you willing to change so that you're not such a "sitting duck"? Remember, behavior that gets rewarded gets repeated. It might be hard to understand *why* your response is a reward to the bully – and you really don't need to – but you can still withdraw the reward. Say the bully seems to get a big kick out of ridiculing you and making others join in the laughter. Try making eye contact, not with the bully, but with one or two others as if to ask "What do *you* think of the way I'm being treated?" Most people will see the bullying for what it is and not participate. Less laughter, less reward. Another thing you can do is to add negative consequences to the interaction. You could add the risk of punishment or ostracizing by making sure responsible co-workers are present whenever you meet the bully.

The more effective a resistance you can put up to the bullying before the pattern of bullying is fully established, the better. You don't necessarily have to defeat the bully; only demonstrate that you're not an easy target.

Document the Bullying

Keeping a log forces you to look at what is happening objectively, which gives you a certain detachment. Objectivity helps you avoid letting the situation get blown out of proportion or, by contrast, minimizing or ignoring it. Seeing the description of the bullying in black and white serves as a continuous reminder that the bully is the one with the problem, not you. Writing down your experiences can also be an emotional release.

Needless to say, keeping a record of the bullying will prove essential if you decide to report the problem to management, or if you choose to discuss it with a counselor. Right now, you may not think it will come to that, but it never hurts to take this precaution. Because of the stress involved in being bullied, targets may be fuzzy about the details about what occurred and when. A log will prove to be an invaluable aid when seeking help. Also, the very act of doing something to help yourself gives you an increased sense of control, which is empowering.

Each log entry should be a description of a bullying incident, including instances when actions of the bully were brought to your attention by others. The description should be fairly brief and should stick to relevant, observable facts. Include the date, time, place, who was present, what the bully said or did, and how you responded. Focus on the behaviors – what was actually said and done – rather than interpreting the events or speculating on the motives. This will not only give you credibility, it will also help to create some distance from the situation and rein in some of the emotions you will undoubtedly feel while being targeted by a bully.

Example (interpretation and speculation):

"Mark, Sandy, Devon, Paul and I got together to plan the warehouse reorganization. Paul was totally out of line and I know it's because he's mad I was made Lead. He kept picking on me, making fun of me and trying to make me look like a fool. I have never been so humiliated in my life. I could tell Sandy thought Paul was being a jerk, too."

Example (objective):

"Marty, Ty, Devon, Paul and I got together to plan the warehouse reorganization. When I was talking, Paul interrupted me, and said 'What would you know about it, Preppy Boy?' He laughed. No one else did. I was embarrassed. When I made another suggestion, Paul said, 'That's idiotic. Why don't you go away and do whatever it is you do, and we'll work it out, okay?'"

Chances are that a few incidents will have already happened before you begin to recognize that you're being bullied. In this case, just record the details as accurately as you can, including the approximate dates. Make a note of the date on which you're making your recollection. The log should also include meetings you may have with a supervisor, Human Resources, a union representative, or other person you go to for help, citing what you reported or requested, how he or she responded, what action was agreed upon, and follow-up actions.

Tips for Writing a Log

- Make an entry for each incident of bullying or disrespectful behavior, as well as meetings with people you go to for help.

- Keep the report fairly brief and to the point.

- Include date, who was bullying and who was present, what disrespectful behaviors were present that contributed to you feeling disrespected, how often, what were the effects on you (how you felt)? Note: Refer to the the Common Bullying Tactics in Chapter 2 to remind you what to call these disrespectful acts.

- Be objective. Avoid interpreting the bully's actions or motives: report what was actually said/done, as opposed to your opinions and "story".

The Bully Free at Work Workplace Bullying Log©

Date/ Time	Location	Bully, People Present	Disrespectful Behavior	How I Felt
8-15	Lunchroom	Marty, Ty, Paul, me	Paul walked by. Bumped me into the vending machines. Kept walking.	Hurt, devalued
8-15	My work station	Paul, Marty, Manny, Ty, Paul, me	Paul started yelling at me, saying I had screwed up the Sure-Fit order. He called me useless and stupid.	Blamed
8-16	My work station	Ty, me	Ty told me Manny in Purch told him Paul said he was really "putting the screws" to "the wimp" (me).	Thwarted, helpless

TIP! Add to the end of your Log "What I Want Instead" of the behavior experienced. This will help give direction to your higher authority—help your boss help you! It becomes a request for behavior change. See page 170 for additional help on this!

Protect Your Health

However you decide to handle the bullying situation, you first need to make sure you're taking care of yourself. In the next chapter, **Take Care of Yourself**, I will talk in detail about taking care of your health. And I will introduce you to a wonderful tool, the Wellness Wheel, that might become your lifelong companion.

Meanwhile, let me just say it is vital that you maintain – or, even better, *improve* – your basic health habits while handling the effects of bullying. Make a special effort to maintain good eating habits. Exercise, at least a little, every day. And make sure to get enough restful sleep. You're already facing challenges in the physical, emotional, mental, social, work and financial aspects of your life. Don't help the bully by letting your defences weaken.

When you are under stress, your body produces a chemical called cortisol. Cortisol increases blood pressure, blood sugar levels, suppresses the immune system, and may even cause infertility in women. Controlling your stress level will effectively block the production of cortisol. By the same token, endorphins – "feel-good", immune system boosting, pain-killing chemicals created by the body – are released when the body exercises. Adopting healthy exercise and stress reduction habits will give you access to all-natural, health-boosting chemicals in your body.

Get Support Right Away

One common and very serious reaction to being bullied is a sense of confusion and self-blame on the part of the target. Sometimes targets will continue trying to sort out what is going on, treating it like a misunderstanding or an interpersonal conflict, so they don't get the support they need right away. They end up feeling isolated, out of control and exhausted. Make sure this doesn't happen to you. Get the emotional support that you need, from family, friends and, if necessary, from a counselor.

Know That You Will Get Through This

Workplace bullying can immediately put you into a state of shock, confusion and panic. "Why does he have it in for me? I don't know how to handle this. What am I going to do?" Before you know it, you can find yourself helplessly reacting, as the situation spins out of control.

You can begin to stop the cycle though, when you get perspective over the situation. You've already made a good start on part of this: acknowledging the bullying; understanding that it is about him, not you; and keeping a record of the bullying.

Now that you've done that however, it's time to start believing that you will definitely get through this. *And that you will be just fine.* Someday – maybe not so far in the future – you will laugh about this, or at least tell entertaining "war stories" about it.

Six strategies for enduring workplace bullying:
(from *Mobbing: Emotional Abuse in the American Workplace*, Davenport, Schwartz and Elliott)

The targets:

1. Figured out what was going on;

2. Responded to the attacks with confidence and without fear;

3. Did not participate in the bullying game (or bullying cycle);

4. Refused to be a victim;

5. Diverted their creative energies from the organization to other pursuits they enjoyed; and

6. Showed much spiritual strength, trusting things would change and stuck it out (or) consciously took steps to leave.[14]

> Everything will be fine in the end. If it's not fine, then it isn't the end.   - Maxine Grey

There's an exercise I know of that works beautifully for me when I'm overwhelmed - when none of my options seem like good ones; when the problem seems so large that I can't see any future beyond it. You may not even feel like this would be worthwhile. You may feel that your situation is really hopeless. That is even more reason to try this - so that you don't feel as stuck. The exercise goes like this…

Exercise: Casting Yourself Forward One Year

> Imagine yourself sitting with a friend, maybe over lunch, one year from now. Invent your conversation, something along this line:

---

14 Davenport et al, 1999. p. 105.

Friend: "You've had quite a year."

You: "I sure have. I never thought I'd survive all that business with (name of the person who is bullying you)."

Friend: "How did that all work out, anyway?"

You: (Describe one possible version of how it was resolved, such as that you eventually confronted the bully and he finally backed down, that Human Resources facilitated a conflict resolution process between you two, that you decided to leave the company, etc.)

Friend: "Oh, so you did do that after all. The last time we talked, you didn't want to take that step."

You: "Yeah, but I realized it was the best thing to do... and it turned out really well."

Friend: "Wow, it must have been scary for you."

You: "Yes, I was scared to death (to stand up to the bully, that you wouldn't be able to get a new job, that your partner wouldn't be supportive, etc.). But it wasn't that hard after all. It's never as bad as you think it might be."

Friend: "And look at you now—you seem so happy....in fact, centered and less stressed - attractive!"

You: "I am. Things worked out a lot better than I thought they would. That doesn't mean things are perfect. (You describe that you and the bully still avoid each other, or that you have a longer commute on your new job, etc.). But it's much better than it was. I don't blame myself; I almost can't believe I did it! Everything is going much better."

Friend: "You know, I admire you very much."

You: "Thanks. I feel pretty proud of myself, too."

I like this exercise - first of all, because the mere image of me sitting with a friend a year from now still in one piece reassures me that I will survive! It pretty much transports me out of the "here and now" that I am finding to be so difficult and overwhelming, and sets me down in a far-off, safe time and place. To hear myself casually chatting about the problem like it is just some tidbit reduces its size and importance enormously. This visualization also allows me to get used to and consider an option that may at first have seemed completely unacceptable. It gives me a chance to pat myself on the back. We can all use a pat on the back sometimes, even if we give it to ourselves.

CHAPTER 6

Take Care of Yourself

> ## Overview
>
> 1. Health and Wellness
>   *Exercise: Wellness Wheel*
> 2. Take Care of Your Physical Health
>   *Assignment: Action Plan to Improve Physical Health*
> 3. Manage Your Stress Level
>   *Assignment: Identify Calming Activities*
>   *Exercise: Reframing Negative Thoughts*
>   *Assignment: Action Plan to Reduce Stress*
> 4. Enlist Support

1. Health and Wellness

The most important thing you can do for yourself is make your overall personal health (wellness) a priority. But what exactly is wellness? Does it just mean not being sick? Being physically healthy? Yes, but it's also more than this. It is about empowering yourself to live a full, rich, healthy, happy life. Wellness is empowerment, and empowerment is wellness.

> **It is about empowering yourself to live a full, rich, healthy, happy life.**

Merriam-Webster defines wellness as "the quality or state of being in good health especially as an actively sought goal."[15] The American Heritage/Stedman Medical Dictionary goes a little further, adding the physical, mental and emotional components of health: "The condition of good physical, mental and emotional health, especially when maintained by an appropriate diet, exercise and other lifestyle modifications."[16] Wikipedia's definition is even more comprehensive, including the concepts of balance and sense of well-being: "In alternative medicine, wellness is generally used to mean a healthy balance of the mind, body and spirit that results in an overall feeling of well-being." [17]

The Wellness Wheel

Wellness pioneer John Travis, M.D., published the Wellness Inventory, a questionnaire that inquires into 12 aspects of your life[18] to help you assess your level of wellness. The wheel is also a good metaphor for the journey through life. The various areas of your life are represented by spokes on a wheel and should be well balanced, and in proper alignment, to enjoy easier steering. Also, the larger your wheel, the more easily you'll be able to roll over "pot holes" in the road of life, barely noticing them. You can see by the example of a completed wheel pictured below that the person is apt to experience a "few bumps" along the way.

There is an abbreviated wellness wheel instrument that was adapted by Wright University from Dr. Travis' instruments and is free of charge to use. This tool has

---

15 http://www.m-w.com/cgi-bin/dictionary?va+wellness
16 The American Heritage® Stedman's Medical Dictionary, 2nd Ed., Houghton Mifflin Company, 2004.
17 http://en.wikipedia.org/wiki/Wellness
18 Eating, breathing, moving, communicating, thinking, playing and working, sensing, feeling, self-responsibility and love, finding meaning, sex and transcending.

seven sections, or "dimensions", as you can see by the illustration below.

The Wellness Wheel

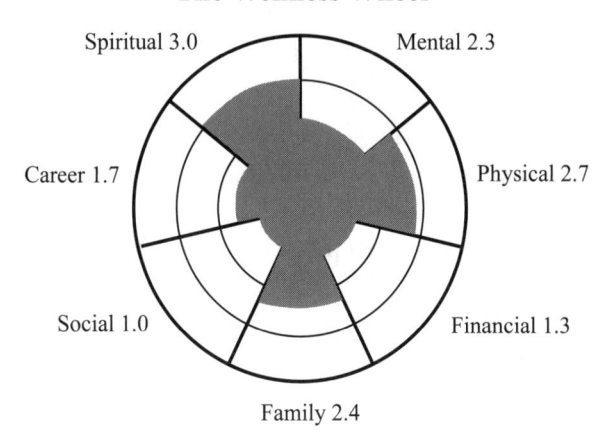

Spiritual 3.0
Mental 2.3
Career 1.7
Physical 2.7
Social 1.0
Financial 1.3
Family 2.4

Exercise: Wellness Wheel

> You can do this exercise by printing out the pages of the abbreviated Wellness Wheel, available at no charge at www.wright.edu/admin/wellness/wellnesswheel.htm. Or you can look at the wellness wheel above and draw it in your journal. Mark the various aspects of the wheel as indicated and then color in at what level you would rate yourself. Coloring right to the outer edge of the circle would indicate satisfaction, with where you are at in this area.
>
> With either version of the Wellness Wheel, score yourself and plot your scores on the wheel.
>
> Look at your wheel. How balanced is it? Any surprises? Now ask yourself what would be your top three areas for improvement. What activities or steps could you take to round out your wheel? Having a full and balanced wheel is really saying that you have a high level of resilience—exactly what you need for self preservation against the effects of bullying.

2. Take Care of Your Physical Health

Many of us let our good health habits slide when we're going through a stressful situation. Just when we need them the most, good nutrition, sleep and exercise habits go by the wayside. Try not to do this. When you're being bullied, you're already being attacked by the bully, so don't make his job easier by further weakening your defences. Fortify yourself as much as you can. The problem may be prolonged, and you'll want to be as energetic and alert as possible so that you can more easily deal with it.

So, how are you taking care of yourself physically? Is there room for improvement?

Assignment: Action Plan to Improve Physical Health

Write "Action plan to improve eating, breathing, moving and sleeping habits" on a blank page in your journal. Write down at least three ways you intend to improve your health habits.

Example: Action plan to improve eating, breathing, moving and sleeping habits

Bring healthy bag lunch 2 times per week.
Eat at least 6 servings of vegetables and fruit every day!
Have no more than one soda per day.
Take 5 minutes out each day for deep breathing.
Climb stairs to office rather than taking elevator.
15 minute stretches every weekday morning. Go to bed by 10pm Sun-Thurs.

3. Manage Your Stress Level

As we saw in Chapter 4, prevailing in a workplace bullying situation requires a four-pronged approach:

1. **State the problem**
   - Acknowledge the bullying.
   - Know that the bullying is about the bully, not you.
   - Understand how bullying affects you.

2. **Protect yourself**
   - Bully-proof yourself.
   - Document the bullying.
   - Protect your health.
   - Know that you will get through this.

3. **Empower yourself**
   - Increase your level of wellness.
   - Take care of your physical health.
   - Manage your stress level.
   - Nurture yourself.
   - Enlist support, have some fun, meditate.
   - Build your self-esteem.
   - Develop your strengths.
   - Increase your options.
   - Build decision-making skills.
   - Learn to assert yourself.

4. **Take action**

At this point, you have already defined the problem and taken steps to protect your health by evaluating your diet, breathing, exercise and sleep habits and establishing an action plan to improve them. Now it's time to address controlling your stress level.

Please understand that controlling your stress level is not the same thing as solving the problem of bullying. Rather, stress is one of your *reactions* to the bullying. Reducing your stress response – in other words, coping more comfortably with what is going on – is crucial to your emotional and physical health. Also, keeping your stress level under control will free you up to deal more effectively with the problem of being bullied.

If we suffered no stress, then bullying wouldn't be a problem at all. We wouldn't need to get support from others. We wouldn't have to learn how to assert ourselves, and increasing our options wouldn't be important. If bullying didn't stress us out so much, we wouldn't have to decide what to do about it. Learning how to release stress is key to handling being bullied, as well as managing other difficult situations in life.

Almost all of the physical, mental, emotional and relationship effects you experience from bullying result from stress. Pay attention to the symptoms of stress, because stress is a cue that something needs to change. If you're being bullied, you'll need to address the core problem; that is, the bullying itself. At the same time, you'll also want to control or minimize the effects of stress on you. If you can manage your stress level, you have the bullying problem half beaten.

> If you can control your stress level, you have the bullying problem half beaten.

The word "stress", to describe tension and strain in humans and other animals, was coined by Dr. Hans Selye, the famous Canadian endocrinologist and author of the classic book, *Stress Without Distress*. Selye's view, now widely accepted, was that we need a certain amount of stress (stimulation) in order to perform at our best. Stress up to that optimal level will dissipate naturally after the need for it is gone. After the race is won, after the exam is finished, after the emergency is handled, then you can relax...

Or can you? Distress, explained Selye, is when you can't relax; when you remain in a state of stress even when the outside cause of stress is gone. The physical, mental and emotional effects remain in your body, leading to chronic ill effects.

> The physical, mental and emotional effects remain in your body, leading to chronic ill effects.

The most common responses to bullying are feeling upset, nervous, increased heart rate, tension, feelings of worry and anxiety and other symptoms of stress. Experienced for a brief time, they are uncomfortable. Experienced for a prolonged period, they can be deadly, leading to serious physical ailments, such as heart disease, ulcers, and vulnerability to disease (review the checklist in Chapter 3 about how bullying is affecting you).

> "Please don't tell me to relax - it's only my tension that's holding me together." - Ashleigh Brilliant

What would you do if a good friend was stressing out? Maybe you would help him to relax, sympathize, let him talk it out, express his worries and fears, steer him gently to get the situation in perspective, and help him see the positives. Why not be a good friend to yourself?

4. Steps to Reducing Stress

Nurture Yourself

What relaxes you, makes you feel comforted, brings you peace of mind? Jogging? A warm bath? A strenuous hike? Listening to music? Lighting a candle?

When in everyday life do you feel the most contented and peaceful—on a bike trail, in your garden, on a neighborhood walk, tinkering in your kitchen or garage, playing with small children or your pet? Being in these peaceful places is, in a way, like meditation. Even though you might be involved in an activity, you lose track of time, you forget about your cares, and you feel contented, calm. When you're under stress, as you are when you're being bullied, that peaceful place or activity can be your haven. It can take you away from your troubles, restore your energy, and help you see the world in a new light.

Assignment: Identify Calming Activities

Write "Activities that bring me peace of mind" on a blank page in your journal. Think about the activities that calm your soul, and write them down. List as many as you can. Try to list at least three or four that you can easily do every day.

Example:
Activities That Bring Me Peace of Mind:
1. Hiking
2. Taking my dog for a walk
3. Cup of tea
4. Warm bath
5. Jazz
6. Massage
7. Meditating/prayer
8. Affirmation tapes

9. Poetry – reading, writing
10. Inspiring movies
11. Talking with Mom
12. Running, working out
13. Being still
14. Gardening
15. Cooking

This list becomes your toolbox for handling stress on a daily basis, so be sure to use it! It may take a bit of effort to actually go through the steps of nurturing yourself in these ways. Sure, it might sound good just to turn on the tube and eat a pint of ice cream (and done occasionally, that won't kill you). Wouldn't it be great though to have a long list of things you can do that will truly calm your mind?

Have Some Fun

Make a special effort – even though you don't feel like it – to have some fun, to laugh. Getting your mind on pleasurable activities will help give you a distance from your workplace woes, and remind you that there is more to your life than just the bullying problem.

Norman Cousins may not have been the first to say "Laughter is the best medicine," but he certainly did prove it. Diagnosed with a terminal illness on top of other life-endangering medical conditions, he set out on a recovery program based on Vitamin C, positive thinking and laughter. His amazing improvement inspired much scientific research, resulting in the identification and study of more than 1000 chemicals in our nervous systems. One of those chemicals is the endorphin, a "feel-good" chemical released when we laugh, play and exercise, bringing a sense of happiness and well-being.

Meditation and Prayer

The sympathetic ear of a friend or loved one can do wonders for our hurt feelings, our wounded pride, the worry we feel about a situation we're facing. Ultimately, though, we're trying to achieve peace of mind. And we can make great strides toward reaching that calm, peaceful place all by ourselves. How? Being still.

Prayer and meditation allow you to stop and get hold of your thoughts. It is really just removing your attention from the bustling world "out there" and directing it to a peaceful place. It's a wonderful way to reduce stress. Don't think that prayer or meditation is a complicated, mysterious practice that takes years to learn. If you want to achieve a calm state of mind and spirit and a calmer sense of well-being, then 15 minutes a day for a few weeks will take you far. Try it for three or four days and see what happens! Everything needs a rest, including you.

Regulate Your Breathing

When we are under stress, our breathing tends to get very shallow, which means we aren't getting enough oxygen. A surprisingly easy way to bring your stress level way down is to adjust your breathing throughout the day. Here is a simple way you can reduce stress very quickly through breathing: Find a quiet place you can sit for five minutes by yourself. Take a long, deep, slow breath in through your nose. Hold it for a count of about five seconds and then release it slowly through your mouth. Do this four times. Then, sit quietly for the balance of the five minutes, breathing in and out deeply, while paying attention to your breath. Do this several times throughout the day if you can.

If you wear a watch with an alarm, set the alarm for an hour or so from now. When it goes off, notice how you are breathing at that moment. If your breathing is not relaxed, do the exercise I've just described.

Avoid "Multi-Tasking"

What an odd word, multi-tasking. To think it has actually become a verb in our world! Some people are proud of the fact that they are good at multi-tasking, which means being able to do several things at one time. I suppose there are circumstances where this is desirable but, mainly, I think multi-tasking is not healthy. Remember, the brain can consciously hold only one thought at a time, so multi-tasking is really moving rapidly back and forth between two or more activities. The danger in multi-tasking is that you can become very scattered, constantly having to reorient yourself as to where you left off with a particular task. You can lose your ability to focus on one thing, complete the operation and then move on to the next one. Ironically, the more stressed we get – when we most need the relative calm of just one task – the more we are inclined to bounce from one activity to another.

Zig Ziglar, famed author and lecturer on goal setting, describes the pitfalls of not having focus by saying that while a person is doing A, they're worried that they should be doing B, so they drop A and race off to do B, until they start worrying they should do C. They can't concentrate on B, so they drop it to go over and start doing C, only to feel, of course, they're neglecting A. They never get A, B or C done – they spend all their time traveling! The failure to accomplish any of the tasks leads to higher stress levels.

Focus on one thing at a time. It may help to draw up a list of tasks you want to complete. This will help keep you on track. The act of crossing out items as you complete them also earns you a satisfying "atta-boy". And don't underestimate the power of small successes for your morale, especially when you're under stress and striving for a feeling of control and accomplishment.

Put a Halt to Negative Self-Talk

Putting a stop to negative self-talk is probably not something you will do overnight. But that's okay. Replacing negative thinking with encouraging thoughts, even if only gradually, will bring you positive results, slowly but surely. When you catch yourself in negative thinking or negative self-talk, notice what that thought is. Then, ask yourself, "How can I reword this in a more positive, but still realistic, term?" As with the breathing exercise above, you can set your watch alarm to go off an hour or two from now and then notice what you're thinking about when it sounds.

Your negative thoughts are not just ideas you made up yourself, you know. They are largely comments people made to you long, long ago, when you were still a child. Remarks that made you feel fearful, not good enough, uncertain, or guilty. They said it; you believed it. These voices still operate as a sort of committee in your head and *you're still listening. You still believe them.* You're being controlled by The Committee. Who is on your committee? What are they saying to you? Try to understand that what they are saying comes from their well-intended but limited thinking, their own view of the world. Just as John Nash, the schizophrenic scientist in the movie "A Beautiful Mind" learned to ignore his committee, you can ignore yours. When they say, "You need to hold onto that job. What if you can't get another one? C'mon, it could be worse. Back in my day...." you can reply, 'Thanks for the input, but I think I'll try something else.'"

Exercise: Reframing Negative Thoughts

Make two columns on a blank page of your journal and write the headings, "Negative Thought" and "Reframed Thought." Write down a negative thought, either just as you become aware of it or later, when you think back on your day. Then, reframe the thought in your mind. What is the real truth about this issue that I'm worried or upset about? The reframed thoughts in my example below are brief, but feel free to expand on the reframed thought as much as you want – you might even want to write an action plan!

Example:

Negative Thought:	Reframed Thought:
I just can't handle this!	This is difficult but I can handle it.
No one cares about me.	Lots of people care about me, especially Jon, Sheila and Sandy.
I'll never be able to pay my bills this month.	I'm scared about my money situation. Let me sit down and work out how I can manage it. Others have; I can, too.

Assignment: Action Plan to Reduce Stress

Review your Wellness Wheel scores and the exercises you've completed and notes you have written about nurturing yourself (identifying the activities that calm your mind), meditating, regulating your breathing, not multitasking, and reframing negative thinking.

Now you're ready to formulate an action plan. Write "Action plan to reduce stress" on a blank page in your journal. You might need to devote two or more pages to this assignment. Write down actions that you will commit to doing in order to reduce your stress level. Ideally, your list will contain something from each of the areas above.

Example:
Action Plan to Reduce Stress

Hiking – Do one evening hike and one day hike a week
Meditate 20 minutes every day, first thing in the morning.
Work out at gym 3 times a week.
Garden 2 hours on the weekend.
Listen to music instead of watching TV one night per week.
Get a massage this week.
Cook a dinner from scratch for yourself or a friend once this week.
Go to bed by 10pm.
Rent a comedy DVD once a week and actually watch it!
Make to-do list each day for next day. Focus on one task at a time.

5. Enlist Support

Hopefully, you have one or more people to whom you can go for support as you handle this experience. If not, you might consider making an appointment with a professional counselor. Another option is to attend a local support group. You should be able to locate such a group through your local hospital and family counselling centers, or by doing an internet search with the terms "support group", and your city's name. Targets of bullying tend to feel isolated, so it's extra important to feel that you have someone on your side. Someone who really understands your situation and is rooting for you.

Chapter 7

Empower Yourself

> ### Overview
>
> 1. Assemble Your Support Team
>   *Assignment: Identifying Your Support Team*
> 2. Build Your Self-Esteem
>   *Exercise: Rosenberg Self-Esteem Scale*
>   *Assignment: Identify Your Strengths*
> 3. Learn How to Make Good Decisions
>   *Assignment: Decision-Making Step #1- Identify Your Options*
> 4. Learn How to Assert Yourself

If you have been working through what we've covered so far – naming the problem, taking stock of how it affects you, seeing where you can improve on how you're taking care of your health, and managing your stress level – then you're well on your way to empowering yourself!

In this chapter, you'll do even deeper work - learning how to get support when you need it, to build your self-esteem, to accept personal responsibility, and to assert yourself.

Recall the four-part approach to dealing with a bullying situation:

1. **State the problem**
   - Acknowledge the bullying.
   - Know that the bullying is about the bully, not you.
   - Understand how bullying affects you.

2. **Protect yourself**
   - Bully-proof yourself.
   - Document the bullying.
   - Protect your health.
   - Know that you will get through this.

3. **Empower yourself**
   - Increase your level of wellness.
   - Take care of your physical health.
   - Manage your stress level.
   - Nurture yourself.
   - Enlist support, have some fun, meditate.
   - Build your self-esteem.
   - Develop your strengths.
   - Increase your options.
   - Build decision-making skills.
   - Learn to assert yourself.

4. **Take action**

Throughout this chapter, we'll be continuing to focus on Step #3 – empowering yourself. You'll be acquiring useful tools to help you through your bullying situation. Some of these tools are exercises that you will do yourself. Others involve enlisting the participation of one or more other people, such as family members or friends. The kind of support you receive will probably differ from one person to another. Try to understand that not everyone is going to meet all of your needs. For example, one person may mainly be able to provide sympathy and emotional support. Another might give you "the pure, unvarnished truth" (whether you like it or not!) and may have some advice to consider. Try to appreciate each person for the particular contributions they can offer without expecting them to be someone other than who they are.

1. Assemble Your Support Team

What is a support team? They are all the people you can count on in your life for support, encouragement and/or guidance. Maybe there are many such people in your life; perhaps only a few. They include not only your family and friends, but also clergy, counselors and other mentors. Your support team may also include acquaintances who, while not close friends, might have insights they are willing to share that will help you deal with the experience you are going through.

Basically, your support team consists of everyone whose help you want and who are willing to give it. Don't wait for people to come up and offer help, even if you think they are aware of the situation. They may not want to intrude, or realize its seriousness. You can always say, "Hey, there is this situation I'm trying to deal with and I would appreciate your advice about it."

> **Your support team consists of everyone whose help you want and who are willing to give it.**

Have you ever tried to reach out to your co-workers or friends to tell them about your workplace bullying situation, but they "weren't there" for you?

Why does this happen? Where is the support? Workplace bullying is hard to battle alone.

The top three reasons why support may not be present for you when you are faced with a workplace bullying situation:

1. They do not know what to do to help; stopping adult bullying is not a topic they know how to coach.

2. They do not realize that simply listening and empathizing can be helpful, even if they do not know what other actions to take.

3. They might not care enough to help. (Most people do/would care if they knew how to help solve adult bullying problems).

Here's what you might experience when you share your workplace bullying situation:

- You are interrupted.

- They don't want to hear you out – they jump in, trying to tell you what to do – they expect you to be able to "fix" your adult bullying situation right away.

- They listen in order to hear gossip, not for your best interests.

- They disagree with your feelings about your adult bullying situation.

- They change the subject frequently or allow themselves to be interrupted.

- They revert the conversation back to themselves: "Oh yeah, that reminds me of the time when…"

- They use condescending statements such as "How is your bullying situation coming along?"

What can you do to secure support to help handle workplace bullying?

1. Choose a friend or co-worker who is kind and a caring, empathetic listener. Who do you know that would fit this bill?

2. Let your friend or co-worker know they do not have to listen in order to solve the problem – you simply want their caring and concern.

3. For advice, seek professional help and guidance. If you choose a therapist, choose someone who has a specialty in conflict resolution and workplace bullying. Ask about their results so far. Make sure you feel comfortable with them.

4. For support at work, ideally you should be able to approach your boss for understanding and protection. If your boss is the bully, you can try an EAP (Employee Assistance Program) or HR (Human Resources) representative. Before approaching these more formal support routes, ask if there is a workplace bullying or adult bullying policy and procedure plan in order to assist a target with adult bullying. You can begin to get a feel for how far you want to take your situation.

5. Last but not least, co-worker support can be very influential and powerful. Having two or more co-workers who are willing to serve as witnesses or support while you take a formal approach to your support needs can be key.

Assignment: Identifying Your Support Team

> Write "My potential support team" on a blank page in your journal. Then sit and brainstorm everyone who might be able to offer some kind of help to you, however minor. You might envision having a heart-to-heart conversation with one member of your support team, and ask for advice on a specfic issue from another.
>
> Another element in having a strong support team is how well you open yourself up to the support that is being offered. For instance, are you comfortable seeking help when you need it, or would you rather "go it alone?" Do you appreciate honest feedback, or does it often make you feel criticized?

"Can We Talk?"

Think about what you would like from the friend you talk to. Sympathy? Empathy? Support? Advice? All three? You probably don't need to be too objective in order to get sympathy. But if you want your friend's help to move forward, you'll need to look at the situation realistically. Only then will she be able to see it realistically. Try not to "horriblize" the situation too much. Avoid casting the person who is bullying you as the villain and yourself as the victim. But the bully is a villain, isn't he? Yes, it's true. He certainly is behaving like one and you're indeed, being victimized by that behavior. But looking at the problem in only villain-and-victim terms doesn't help you solve the problem. Instead, it keeps you in an endless loop of "you won't believe what he did to me today" conversations with your friend. When you've finished describing the problem in its worst terms, you'll feel even more helpless and discouraged. Your friend will feel powerless to help and perhaps a growing frustration at your willingness to complain about it but not to do anything about it.

Does that mean you can never feel sorry for yourself and look to your supportive friend for sympathy? No, not at all. But your friend needs to know what it is you want from her. Being clear about this will help you get the support and guidance you need.

A colleague told me about a technique she came up with that turned out to be a godsend when her young daughter would bring up upsetting problems at school. Before her breakthrough, my friend had simply been asking a casual "Hi honey, how was your day?" only to suddenly find herself in a tempest of drama and turmoil. She had tried responding with sympathy, agreement or advice, but usually found her failure to guess the "right" reply only further upset and frustrated the daughter. ("Never mind. I don't know why I even brought it up!") Then my friend came up with an idea. She told her daughter she was happy to talk with her about her day at school, but she needed to know what the girl wanted. She asked her daughter to say one of three things:

> "Can I feel sorry for myself out loud for a minute?"
> "Can I complain for a minute?"
> "Can I ask your advice?"

If her daughter asked the first question, she would know to offer sympathy and sympathy only. She let the girl know she understood and cared how she felt. If the girl asked the second question, they would play "ain't he awful" for a few minutes, exaggeratedly agreeing what a terrible person the subject of the discussion was. The daughter could thus vent her sense of indignation in this safe environment without having to worry about being fair or objective. If

129

her daughter asked the third question, she gave advice. She was supportive, but objective and not overly sympathetic.

This worked like a charm. Not only did her daughter get what she needed, but she became clearer about what she really wanted when she came for help. It also made her conscious about *when* she was feeling sorry for herself or complaining, and so thus avoided getting stuck in those feelings for too long. A little can be good. A lot is not so good!

There was also another important benefit. Before they started this approach, just the mother's cheerful "Hi honey, how was your day?" might unleash a torrent of complaints that Mom was not always emotionally prepared for. (After all, *she* might have had a hard day, too). Now, she was being asked, which made all the difference. She could say "Sure, honey. What's going on?" or "Of course. But let's wait until we get home, okay? Right now, I need a few minutes of peace and quiet."

When you talk with your friend then, try to be clear about what you want. Is it sympathy? Maybe you want to vent a little, complain, get it off your chest? Do you want advice? Communicate with your friend what you want. ("Hey, I could really use some sympathy right now – got about 5 minutes?") If you're ready to move on to asking for guidance, or would like a sounding board for an action you're thinking about taking, let your friend know. ("Thanks a lot. That makes me feel a lot better. Maybe you could tell me what you think about…") Don't take your friend for granted, thinking she is always ready and willing to listen to you. Tell your friend you'd like to talk for a specified amount of time, i.e., 1 minute, 2 minutes, 5 minutes; and make it a request. Lastly, show your appreciation for her willingness to be a friend to you.

2. Build Your Self-Esteem

Most people who have suffered as a result of an interaction (or many interactions) with someone very difficult will want to call their experience "bullying". The severity of the experience is directly linked to one's level of self esteem at the time.

If you're experiencing bullying behavior, it might seem – even to you – that it's because you're afraid to stand up to the bully. And that may be true. But there may be a second reason that you endure this treatment. Down deep, you may not expect more respectful treatment. You may not value yourself as highly as you could, and suspect that the bullying is justified, that you don't deserve more respect.

We all get down on ourselves from time to time. That's very normal. But there are some who just don't appreciate themselves as much as they could. Do you often feel like a failure, useless, not as important as others? If you do, then you probably have low self-esteem. So when others make critical and hurtful remarks to you, you hurt doubly. Once because the person making the insult believes it is true. Twice because you believe it yourself.

How would you rate your self-esteem? In **Chapter Six**, the *Mental and Spiritual* sections of the abbreviated Wellness Wheel reflect your level of self-esteem, as do the *Feeling, Communicating and Finding Meaning* dimensions of the Wellness Inventory.

Does your score indicate low self-esteem is an issue for you? As well as the Wellness Wheel, I have included another simple self-test you can do to measure your self-esteem. Developed by Dr. Morris Rosenberg, who is renowned for his work in self-concept, the Rosenberg Self-esteem Scale is probably the most widely used scale to measure self-esteem in both adolescents and adults.

Exercise: Rosenberg Self-Esteem Scale

1. Below is a list of statements dealing with your general feelings about yourself. Consider each statement and, without thinking too long about your response, decide if you strongly agree, agree, disagree or strongly disagree. Then circle the corresponding number.
2. When you're finished, total up the numbers. Your total should be between 0 and 30.

Rosenberg Self-Esteem Scale		Strongly Agree	Agree	Disagree	Strongly Disagree
1.	I feel that I'm a person of worth, at least on an equal plane with others.	3	2	1	0
2.	I feel that I have a number of good qualities.	3	2	1	0
3.	All in all, I am inclined to feel that I am a failure.	0	1	2	3
4.	I am able to do things as well as most other people.	3	2	1	0
5.	I feel I do not have much to be proud of.	0	1	2	3
6.	I take a positive attitude toward myself.	3	2	1	0
7.	On the whole, I am satisfied with myself.	3	2	1	0
8.	I wish I could have more respect for myself.	0	1	2	3
9.	I certainly feel useless at times.	0	1	2	3
10.	At times I think I am no good at all.	0	1	2	3
	Total score = _____				

> ### Interpreting the Rosenberg Self-Esteem Scale
> Dr. Rosenberg did not use specific cut-off points to designate low, average and high self-esteem. I feel that a score of 18 or below indicates low self-esteem, 19 to 25 indicates average self-esteem, and 26 and above indicates high self-esteem.

Many of us suffer, or have suffered in the past, from low self-esteem. If you have low self-esteem this means you undervalue yourself. Another way of looking at this is *your actual worth is more than you think*. The roots of low self-esteem go back to childhood, when you were impressionable to what others said to and about you, especially the people closest to you. How you perceived what they said and did in some way made you come to the decision that you weren't smart, or good-looking, or strong, or athletic, or…the list goes on.

But that was then, and this is now. The good news is, whatever the origins of your insecurities, there is much you can do to boost your self-esteem and confidence.

One of the themes I have expressed throughout this book is understanding that the bully's behavior is about the bully, not about you. I've also stressed the importance of getting some distance (perspective) from the bullying. This is extremely difficult to accomplish if your self-esteem is so low that you accept the bully's demeaning comments as truth.

If low self-esteem is a problem for you, I truly hope you will make it a priority to build your self-esteem. Not only will you be able to shrug off the bullying with much greater ease, you will also be able to continue through life with the self-respect and confidence that you deserve.

Self-Esteem and Personal Responsibility

An important part of self-esteem is accepting personal responsibility in one's life. Does this sound like a scary notion to you? That's not surprising. Personal responsibility can be a hard idea to accept because responsibility is so often mistaken for blame. People who feel blamed and criticized often are likely to resist the notion of taking personal responsibility for a particular situation. After all, it sounds a lot like they are being blamed *again*.

Personal responsibility means accepting accountability for your words and actions (and inactions) and understanding their influence in daily life. Responsibility is acknowledging that one's actions (or inactions) may well influence the outcome of a situation. Blame – either directed at oneself or at others – is laying the entire fault for an outcome, not on words or deeds, but on a person or people. Even people who are generally quite self-responsible may avoid acknowledging responsibility in areas that they feel particularly insecure about. They already feel blamed about this issue and have a strong need to feel that this was in no way "their fault."

For those of you who feel blamed and criticized a lot, it's extra important for you to develop your sense of personal responsibility. Rather than deepen your feelings of guilt, shame and resentment, it will actually help *release* you from them. Why? Because you are not your actions. You can do something unkind and still be a good person. When you accept personal responsibility, you can evaluate your actions more objectively because you don't feel like you're being personally attacked. You can then decide what you might do to remedy the situation or what you might do differently next time. Because you have newfound control, you won't feel so victimized by others.

People who blame others do so because, down deep, they feel at fault. They have to blame someone else, because otherwise they think they would have to admit to themselves that they are not a good enough person. So you see, there is really no difference between a person who excessively blames and one who feels excessively blamed.

People who would say they accept "too much" personal responsibility are actually blaming themselves too much or covering for someone else who needs to accept more responsibility. So do you accept "too much" or not enough personal responsibility?

Focus on Your Strengths

What are your strengths? Strengths are qualities that we and others can appreciate and admire about ourselves. There are personality and character strengths, such as friendliness, patience, kindness, honesty, loyalty, dependability, intelligence, sense of humour and an even temperament. Physical characteristics might include nice eyes, a great smile, a fit figure, beautiful hair or physical stamina. Special talents and aptitudes can run from A to Z. Maybe you're a great dancer, have a green thumb, are a good cook, have an interesting hobby, or are one of those people who can fix anything with a paper clip and duct tape. Or perhaps you have a special love for animals, nature or the sea. Maybe you are a person who listens to others well.

All of these traits are gifts given to you so you can enjoy life more fully – and so that you can share them with others. There isn't another person on this earth who has exactly the same gifts as you. They are what make you unique and special. The following quotation is attributed to Henry Ford: "Try to leave this world a better place when you depart it than when you entered." What ideas can you use to benefit others? What are you involved in that is bigger than yourself? Are you leaving a You-shaped hole in the world?

> What ideas can you use to benefit others?

For some, the lower one's self-esteem, the more they will not acknowledge the talents and gifts of others - especially if they are talents and gifts that they wished they themselves possessed. They envy and maybe even feel jealous that someone else runs 10Ks.

Yet almost all of us tend to take for granted our own positive traits and talents, thinking "Big deal, so I'm a decent photographer. Anyone could do it if they wanted to…" (which isn't true). The lower your self-esteem, the more you'll tend to discount or completely overlook wonderful qualities that you have. And that others may be admiring and secretly envying!

> "No one can make me feel inferior without my permission". — Eleanor Roosevelt

Assignment: Identify Your Strengths

The first step in focusing on and building your strengths is, of course, to identify them.

1. At the top of a blank page of your journal, write "My Strengths", then make three headings, "Personality and Character Traits," "Physical Characteristics," and "Talents and Aptitudes," leaving enough space after each heading to fill in details. (See example below.)
2. Next, make up a similar form on a blank of sheet of paper and make several photocopies. Give these copies to people who know you well, and ask them to complete it. Let them know you're working on a project for your self-reflection. Ask them to take the worksheet with them and complete it when they can devote a little time to thinking about it. Emphasize that it is their honest opinions that will be of most help to you.
3. Consider the headings on the "My Strengths" page in your journal, and taking a few days to reflect, write down what you think your strengths are. Write down even those qualities that you think are "no big deal." Remember, all of us and especially people with low self-esteem tend to discount our good points.
4. When you've gotten the worksheets back, compare those observations with your own. Are there some differences? Do others notice and appreciate strengths in you that you yourself don't see?
5. Add your family's and friend's observations to your own list.
6. Set aside some time and really consider the qualities that others and you recognize in you. Do this often. And always feel free to add more strengths as they occur to you!

Example:

My Strengths:

Personality and character traits:	
• Honest • Caring • Responsible • Smart • Hard-working • Loyal • Patient • Fun-loving	• Good listener • Dependable • Good sense of humour • Open-minded • Flexible • Disciplined (determined) • Tidy • Methodical
Physical Traits:	
• Nice smile/nice face • Good health/rarely sick • Takes care of self	• Strong/has endurance • Good eye contact • Lots of energy
Talents and Aptitudes:	
• Good cook • Likes to entertain • Handy around the house • Plays guitar well • Sings pretty well	• Wide range of interests • Good outdoors person • Athletic – run, ski, bike • Great storyteller • Good with kids & animals
Personal Gifts to Share, Develop and Acquire:	
• Caring/patient/great storyteller – volunteer at a senior's center? • Fun-loving/good cook/entertain – have friends over more? • Good listener – get closer with Dave. • Handy around the house – make to-do list and get busy! • Good with kids – have niece and nephew over more often. • Good with animals – volunteer at an animal shelter?	

Improve Your Options

One of the thoughts you might have when you're being bullied is "There's nothing I can do about this. I can't afford to lose this job." Think about how powerful you'd feel if you *could* afford to give up your job and move on. You may not choose to do it, but at least it would be an option. Then if the bullying continues, you wouldn't feel so helpless.

3. Learn How to Make Good Decisions

I've often thought that the biggest mistake people seem to make when it comes to making decisions is in the timing. They either make the decision too soon or too late. Let me explain.

Making a decision too soon – that is, starting now and continuing to mull over a decision for maybe months until it's *really* time to make it – is like deciding which fork in the road you'll take long before you get to the fork. Until you get there, you don't know what the two roads are like and whether or not there will be sign posts to guide you. If you're not ready to choose an option, don't use up your valuable time and emotional energy speculating, brooding about what you think your choices will be. And if this sounds a lot like worrying, that's because making a decision before its time is worrying. Maybe this will happen, maybe that will happen... And *maybe* it won't. Most of the things we worry about never even happen.

> Most of the things we worry about never happen.

If you're being bullied, naturally you're going to be thinking about the different ways it could turn out. This can be

139

helpful, preparing you mentally and emotionally for change. Thinking generally about your options is also good, and doing what you can to increase and improve them is very positive. Before it's time to make the decision, you should be engaged in identifying your options and improving them. Keep your attention focused on handling today well, which will improve your options.

On the other end, some people don't make a decision until after their options have seriously eroded. This is usually due to fear, which is understandable. Sometimes they have frightened themselves into "analysis paralysis" by worrying about all the bad ways the situation could turn out.

Another common reason people put off making a decision is that they aren't sure which one of the options is "the" right one. Usually though, there isn't just one right option. There are several that would work just fine. Since you don't have a crystal ball, you can only make your decision based on the information that you have *at this point in time.*

Three Steps to Good Decisions

After you have stated the problem, as you have already done in Chapter 5, **So What Can You Do?**, there are three steps to making good, solid decisions:

1. **Identify your options:**
   This is the brainstorming step. When brainstorming options, you write down every possibility you can think of, including variations on the options. You don't evaluate the alternative solutions at this point because that would stop the creative flow of ideas. Get the input of your support team to create a list of possibilities.

2. **Evaluate the options:**
   In this step, you'll evaluate each alternative solution. Write down the pros and cons of this option, based on the information you have at this time. Underline or add a star next to the advantages and disadvantages that are especially significant to you. If there are obstacles attached to a certain option, note it. For instance, obstacles for the option of looking for a new job might be "outdated resume" and "don't have enough savings".

3. **Choose an option:**
   Pick the option that seems to be the best fit. If the option has one or more obstacles associated with it, write down how you will handle the obstacle(s). For example, you might write, "Begin looking for a new job. To do: Update resume; save 3 months' pay."

Assignment: Decision-Making Step #1
- Identify Your Options

Go to the "Statement of Problem/Options" page in your journal. Write down every option (and variation) you can think of. Don't evaluate them yet; just keeping writing whatever comes into your mind. Talk with your support team and get their ideas, too. I will ask you to come back and complete Steps #2 and #3 a little later.

Example:
Statement of Problem:

Who: Paul Harwood

What/How Often: Makes fun of me in front of others by pre-calling poor job performance on my part; not giving me specific deadlines and then saying I was late turning in my project. Each time I've been in contact this past week, an incident such as above has occurred.

The Effects: This is causing me insomnia; and it is hard to concentrate on my job. I also feel left out and demoralized, and am beginning to doubt my own abilities.

<u>Step #1</u>: Identify Your Options
1. Ignore him.
2. Avoid him.
3. Try harder to get along with him.
4. Talk to him – what is the problem?.
5. Talk to him – ask him to lay off.
6. Threaten to report him.
7. Talk to supervisor.
8. Talk to HR – get advice.
9. Talk to HR – report him.
10. Write note to Paul – ask him to lay off.
11. Ask for transfer out of Warehouse.
12. Campaign – assert myself at every encounter.
13. Look for another job.
14. Take legal action against company.

4. Learn How to Assert Yourself

People either tend to behave in a passive, aggressive or assertive way; based on the situation and their level of self confidence in a given situation. Assertiveness is not just midway between extreme passivity and aggression; it is the healthy alternative to both. Neither extreme passivity nor aggression is healthy or respectful. The person who displays passive tendencies has a lack of respect for his or her own rights and places a higher value on others' rights. The person who appears more aggressive, on the other hand, respects his or her own rights but disrespects the rights of others. Both will generally harbor resentful or disdainful feelings about the other (also not very respectful).

> Passive: I respect you, but not myself.
> Aggressive: I respect myself, but not you.
> Assertive: I respect myself and you.

Assertiveness, however, is a respect for one's own needs and rights as well as the needs and rights of others. People who are assertive communicate their feelings honestly and respectfully. Because they are honest and upfront, you know where you stand with them. It is important to people who are assertive to have their needs met, but not at the expense of others. They accept personal responsibility for themselves but do not accept responsibility for others. They don't hold their feelings in, therefore they don't let frustration build up.

> **People who are assertive accept personal responsibility for themselves, but do not accept responsibility for others.**

Achieving assertiveness is a step-by-step process and is closely linked with personal responsibility. Most of us lean, at least slightly, toward being passive or being aggressive until we really make the commitment to become an assertive person who respects the needs of ourselves and others. A person who leans toward passivity will have to overcome a deeply entrenched desire to be thought of as "nice", a fear of confrontation, perhaps a sensitivity to criticism, and other self-doubts. A person who tends to be more aggressive will have to learn self-restraint, maybe reverse a deep-seated notion that he or she is better than others, and develop empathy for others. Both will need to learn how to communicate honestly and caringly.

We'll talk much more about assertiveness skills in Chapter 8, **Handling the Bully**.

Chapter 8

Handling the Bully

Overview

1. Things You Can Do Now to Stop the Impact of Bullying
2. Minor Bullying
3. Moderate-Level Bullying
   Self-Test: How Assertive Are You?
   Assignment: Responding Assertively
   Assignment: Daily Debriefing
4. Severe Bullying
5. Prepare to Leave, Even If You Don't
   Assignment: Preparing to Leave
   Assignment: Decision-Making Step #2 - Evaluate Your Options
   Assignment: Decision-Making Step #3 - Choose an Option

How you deal with the bully will depend on the severity of the behavior, how it is affecting you, and on your particular situation (how important the job is to you, what options you have, etc.). Bullying can be a minor problem, a moderate-level problem, or a severe problem. Ask yourself: How bad is the bullying? Does it look like it's getting worse? How much contact do I have with this person? How much does the bullying bother me? How is it affecting me, physically and emotionally? Is it creating stress in my life? How important is this job to me? How important is this company to me? How do I feel about transferring to another department; is that even an option? If it comes to leaving, how easily can I get a good job somewhere else? What is my financial situation?

1. Things You Can Do Now to Stop the Impact of Bullying

If you did not feel rejected, disrespected and thwarted from the bully, then there would not really be a problem. The question then remains: What can one do to stop the effects one feels as a result? Would you be open to realizing that there may be some things you are doing (but you can have control over) that may be attracting the bully?

Here are some things to consider for people who feel they are the target of a bully:

1. Some targets have trouble asserting themselves at the best of times. Fear of rejection drives the target's inaction.

   What to do: Study assertiveness. Know you have the right to say something (if you choose). Experiment where the challenge is not as tough. Try it once – the sun will still come out tomorrow!

2. Some targets have a challenge in making decisions on what they want instead. Most of us know what we don't want and we can easily explain the problem.

   What to do: Make a list of "What I don't want". On the other side of the page, articulate "What I want instead". Then decide what you want, and will/won't do. Pick a lane – it will be freeing. Again, try this for small wins first. It will give you energy, clarity and ultimately power.

3. Some targets stuff their anger and put on a "pleasant face". Stuffing anger occurs for many reasons, but know you have the right to be angry; it does not make you a bad person. What you do with your anger is key…and in your control.

   What to do: Specifically ask a friend or confidant to "hear you out for two minutes, with no interruptions". You get to say anything you want. Your listener has an open body position to listen to your expression of the anger. They do not have to solve your challenge, only receive it, i.e., hear it. A big part of anger management is feeling heard. Try it – you are best to channel these emotions elsewhere, rather than trapping them in your body or avoiding them.

Why do we tend to not want to deal with our anger? One reason is that we still try to convince ourselves that "it isn't that bad and I can handle this", or we feel that we are "supposed to handle this – better". Remember, you are only human.

4. Some targets tend to put others' needs first.

   What to do: Ask yourself "What do I need?". Try this for one hour, then you can go back to thinking about others.

5. Some targets need the approval of others in order to feel valued. When someone doesn't like you, it is hard to rest until the mystery is solved.

   What to do: Know that 10% of the people won't like you anyway – for their own reasons, which have nothing to do with you. You may be better at something, or have more of something, etc. This is called envy, which says more about the bully than it does about you.

2. Minor Bullying

Would you say it is minor bullying, or really just an annoyance? That it bothers you a little right when it happens but then you easily forget about it? Maybe the person bullies others, too. Or possibly you're new and the bully is testing you, like he does with all newcomers. If the behavior isn't upsetting you, isn't affecting your work, and doesn't seem to be escalating, then you might consider it minor. But if the bullying itself is fairly trivial but is seriously affecting you, it is not minor.

What is and isn't minor bullying is subject to interpretation. Generally though, the bullying may take the form of teasing and arguing, rather than explicit insults and yelling.

The behavior of the bully is experienced by most as difficult. With clear, confident and accountable conversations, this behavior may change. If a target does not say anything and proceeds to let this behavior get the best of them, this mild bullying behavior, unaddressed, may unnecessarily grow into dissonance.

Your approach? Use your influence.

Why Should <u>You</u> Be the One to Change?

Why are you the one reading this book about bullying – shouldn't it be the bully reading it? Shouldn't it be the bully who changes instead of you? Yes, of course. The bully should definitely make changes. But that doesn't mean she will, at least not voluntarily. So, if you want things to be different, you will need to lead the change.

Skills and Tools to Handle Minor Bullying:

- Acknowledge the bullying.
- Bully-proof yourself.
- Protect yourself.
- Manage your stress level.
- Build your self-esteem.
- Empower yourself.

You're already acquainted with the skills and tools you need in order to handle minor bullying. You know the importance of acknowledging the bullying (stating the problem) to help you maintain a healthy perspective about what is happening. You understand the importance of keeping a record of the bullying, in case you should ever need it. You know about bully-proofing yourself so you don't present such a tempting target. You've learned the importance of protecting your health, by practicing good nutrition, exercise and sleep habits. You've been introduced to the concept of wellness, or self-empowerment, which means peak functioning in all areas of your life. You've learned about personal empowerment, which includes the ability to manage your stress easily. It also consists of strong self-esteem and a good support network.

Hopefully, your awareness of these skills and your understanding about how important they are to handling a bully will motivate you to practice and ultimately master them.

3. Moderate-Level Bullying

Moderate-level bullying is a serious problem. At this level, the bully is consistent. There is nothing offhand about it; he has you in his crosshairs.

The bully's behavior is experienced by most people as very difficult. Should the target have good boundaries and stronger self esteem, there is a chance of influencing the bully's behavior through discussions based in clarity, confidence and accountability.

The behavior of the bully is experienced by the target as either severe if the target's self esteem is weaker, or as moderate if the target's self esteem is stronger.

To handle him, you'll need to use all of the skills I've described for handling minor bullying. But these won't be enough. You'll also need to enlist support from family and friends, and possibly assert yourself with the bully.

Your approach: Influence (if your confidence is stronger).
                Intervention (if your confidence is lower).

> Skills and Tools to Handle Moderate-Level Bullying:
>
> - Acknowledge the bullying.
> - Bully-proof yourself.
> - Protect yourself.
> - Manage your stress level.
> - Build your self-esteem.
> - Empower yourself.
> - Enlist support.
> - Assert yourself with the bully.

Enlisting Support

You've already learned about how to get support from family and friends in Chapter 7, **Empower Yourself**. You've also learned how to clarify for yourself what kind of support you need (sympathy or advice) and how to ask for it.

Speaking Up to the Boss: The Top Fears

You want to speak up to the bully, but you are not sure what to say. You end up by not saying anything. Now what?

Speaking up to a bully is a lot like surfing, i.e., 90% paddling and 10% riding the wave. There is a lot of preparation and confidence building needed in order to be effective. Dealing with a bully constitutes the same rationale – you want to be effective, so you prepare until you feel that you are.

When it comes to dealing with a bully boss, your main feeling is fear. Here are some of the top fears – "If I say something to the bully...":

Fear: You keep wondering and doubting if the behavior you are experiencing is in fact bullying behavior.

What Happens: Most "nice" people want to see the best in others, and they often have a hard time justifying a confrontation with anyone. There is a small part of themselves that wonders "What if I'm wrong?"

What to Do: In order to gain conviction and assurance that you are experiencing bully behavior, document the situations that occur. This will remind you that you have the right to say something. P.S. Remember your approach does not have to be harsh – but it does need to be firm.

Fear: You are worried that once you speak up, the bully will treat you even worse.

What Happens: True, the bully will likely push back – expect this. But what does this really mean? If targets can expect this and remind themselves that the bully's control needs are about the bully and not the target, then the target can perhaps hang in there. Eventually many a bully will see you are strong and that you can assert a boundary. They may move on to an easier target.

What to Do: Hang in there - consistently standing up for yourself, documenting, and speaking the facts as you see them.

Fear: Once the bully retaliates, you are not sure what to say.

What Happens: This prevents you from saying anything at all.

What to Do: Less is more, and it shows confidence. Be aware that after stating what you need to say, clearly and with confidence, the bully will likely push back. Be ready to minimize their hostility and need for control with short, simple, come-back phrases (see Chapter 9: **Short Simple Come-Backs to Use with Bullies**).

Asserting Yourself

Once you evaluate the bullying behavior, its frequency and its impacts, the next step is to determine what you want, as opposed to what you are currently experiencing.

Most people, when faced with a behavior that they do not want to be around, know what they *don't* want (they can express what the bully does); but they don't know what they *do* want instead. Deciding what you want to see instead makes you a leader in moving toward a solution.

Non-assertiveness, or passivity, invariably leads to high stress and low self-esteem. People who are passive are motivated mainly by a strong need to be accepted, and to be liked. They have difficulty saying "no", they are forever trying to please others, and they especially don't want anyone to be angry or hurt. They tend to take care of everyone but themselves.

It's no wonder then that when people choose to be passive, they store up a lot of frustration and resentment. Their own needs are not being met. They may bottle up their frustration for a long time, until it finally explodes out in damaging, aggressive ways. If they attempt to relieve the growing tension along the way, it is usually through other unhealthy means, such as overeating or depending too much on alcohol or drugs for comfort. They might also seek validation for their hurt feelings from sympathetic friends by chronically complaining and gossiping about the ill-doer. This is all right in small doses, but it's unhealthy when the person habitually complains instead of taking steps to correct the problem.

> **Stress is what happens when your gut says "No" and your mouth says, "Of course, I'd be glad to."**
> **- Unknown**

Remember, people who are passive respect others but not themselves. People who are aggressive respect themselves but not others. People who are assertive respect themselves *and* others.

Self-Test: How Assertive Are You?

Consider each of the following statements, then circle the number under the phrase that most closely describes your attitude about it.

How Assertive Are You?	Strongly Agree/ Always	Agree/ Often	Disagree/ Not often	Strongly Disagree/ Never
1. You feel tense if someone is angry or upset, even if it's not your fault.	0	1	2	3
2. You can usually say "no" to someone without feeling guilty.	3	2	1	0
3. You often feel that others take advantage of you.	0	1	2	3
4. You find it easy to take responsibility for a problem.	3	2	1	0
5. You often feel hurt that your partner or friend isn't considerate about your needs.	0	1	2	3
6. You are able to constructively express feelings of anger or frustration to someone close to you, rather than holding the feelings in.	3	2	1	0
7. You often make excuses to get out of doing something you don't feel like doing.	0	1	2	3

How Assertive Are You?	Strongly Agree/ Always	Agree/ Often	Disagree/ Not often	Strongly Disagree/ Never
8. You always stand up for yourself firmly, but respectfully, if someone "crosses the line" with you.	3	2	1	0
9. You hate confrontations.	0	1	2	3
10. You see yourself as strong and independent.	3	2	1	0
11. You feel blamed and criticized by others.	0	1	2	3
12. You find it easy to make decisions and you trust your own judgment.	3	2	1	0
13. You feel that people who are assertive are arrogant and superior.	0	1	2	3
14. When it comes to relationships, you feel there is a good balance of give and take.	3	2	1	0
15. You envy others who seem more powerful than you.	0	1	2	3

<u>Interpreting the assertiveness self-test</u>

The highest possible score is 45. If your score is between 0 and 18, your tendency is to handle situations very passively (non-assertively). If your score is between 19 and 32, you handle yourself fairly assertively, probably more so in some situations and not so much in others. If your score is between 33 and 45, you don't seem to have any problems asserting yourself.

If you tend to be passive, you're not alone. Becoming assertive takes work. You may have heard the joke about the tourist in New York, who asked a local, "How do you get to Carnegie Hall?" The New Yorker answered, "Practice! Practice! Practice!" *And that's how you get to assertiveness, too.*

> Assertiveness takes practice, practice, practice.

Don't confuse aggressiveness with assertiveness. Remember that assertiveness respects your rights and the rights of others. Going from allowing yourself to be picked on to finally "standing up for yourself" by getting even with the person is not assertive. It is aggressive. Perhaps you feel you have often been taken advantage of by a particular person. Or maybe she takes you for granted or otherwise treats you poorly. Chances are she does it because you let her. In a way, you're giving your permission, so don't hold her 100% responsible. Don't waste your time feeling resentful, or holding it in until you blow up in anger. We can also waste a lot of extra time wondering "why she is/was incapable of seeing what I need". (Or secretly delighting when she suffers some misfortune, saying to yourself, "It serves her right.") Instead, start responding more assertively in your encounters with her. Treat both her and yourself with respect. Then you'll both win.

The Process of Becoming Assertive

The process of becoming assertive is very simple. Simple, but not easy. Just remember that being assertive means respecting your own needs and rights, and respecting other people's rights. Becoming assertive requires practicing this principle over and over. And over again. You'll forget.

You'll be intimidated. You'll get tongue-tied. That's okay. You will get better at it, inch by inch. Life will become easier, more satisfying. Just keep your feet moving.

> *A story is told about monks who were subjected to a test by being put into a dark room, one by one, and instructed to go across the room and open the door on the other side. In this room, they were told, their very worst fears would seem to appear before them, but that the images were just illusions, the invention of their own imaginations. Monk after monk would try but then give up, screaming in horror, and would have to be removed from the room. Finally, after quite a while in the room, one monk opened the door on the other side and walked out, unscathed. The older monks asked him how he did it, and he replied, "As I saw horrible images and felt terrifying things bump up against me, I reminded myself that they were not real. And I knew that I would eventually get to the door, even though I didn't know where it was, if I just kept my feet moving..."*

Just remember to keep your feet moving.

You don't have to know the "right" path to take. You will take detours and make wrong turns. That's all okay. Just keep your feet moving. When you wake up every day, just say to yourself, "Today is a new day and I'm going to keep my feet moving on the path to becoming an assertive, happy human being."

Which Came First: The Behavior or the Belief?

The largest obstacle you will encounter along your journey toward assertiveness will be your self-doubts - your deeply ingrained feelings that you don't have the right to have your needs met. And why are these feelings so ingrained? Because you've been saying them over and over to yourself for an awfully long time now.

When you're afraid to stick up for yourself, say to yourself, "I have the right to ----." Keep saying it. However, don't wait until the negative self-chatter completely goes away before you act. That may never happen.

Assignment: Responding Assertively

- Think of at least five incidents you have been involved in with another person, in which you responded passively (or aggressively) after which you had hurt or angry feelings. It's better if the incidents don't all involve the same person. It doesn't matter if the exchange happened recently or long ago. Consider interactions with co-workers, your boss, friends, family members, and people you meet incidentally throughout the day, such as store clerks and people you pass on the hiking trail. Also think of the bullying situation you may be in.

- For each incident, write a brief description of (1) what the other person did or said that bothered you, and (2) how you responded.

- Then, think about and write down how you might have responded more assertively.

Example:

(Other person):	"How many times are you going to ask the same question?" (said in a condescending tone)
Me (actual response):	"Sorry."

| Me (assertive response): | "Yes, actually I'm new to this – I'll try and get it as best as I can. I appreciate your help." (Note: this is neither defensive, resentful or pushy. It acknowledges the other person while not backing down). |

Learning to Take Control of Your Life

Becoming assertive is not so much about taking a dramatic stand on big issues as it is about continuing to respond assertively dozens of times about small issues throughout your day. Reclaiming your power starts with noticing when you are giving away your power by going along with other people's choices (usually through habit). You can progress quickly if you make it a routine to have a conversation with yourself about the encounters you have every day, and record your thoughts in your journal.

Up until now, whenever you would get a nagging feeling that someone was taking advantage of you, or you felt pressured to do something you didn't want to, or someone made a biting remark that you let slide by, what would you do? How would you feel? Powerless? Victimized? Did you feel bad about the situation? Bad about yourself? Bad (resentful) about the other person? From now on, put these experiences to work for you. You will probably find yourself "going along" quite often for awhile. Remember, it's a deeply ingrained habit, so be patient with yourself! For instance, let's say your friend suggests that you rent a movie tonight. Without thinking, you automatically agree, even though you really would have preferred to go out. Instead of feeling powerless in this situation and perhaps resentful of your friend for always being the one who gets to choose, remind yourself that you also made a choice. Your choice was *not to choose*, but to go along. Re-run the dialogue in your head and, this time, rehearse a different response. Every time you handle a situation the old (non-assertive) way, rehearse handling it in a new (assertive) way. Little by little, you will replace the old behaviors with the new.

Assignment: Daily Debriefing

> Make it a daily practice to review the encounters you had today. Repeat the Responding Assertively exercise you just finished. What did the other person do or say? How did you respond? How might you have responded in a more assertive way, one that respects yourself and the other person? Be easy on yourself – you're just learning this skill!
>
> This will do two amazing things for you in your journey to becoming assertive. First, it will remind you of the basic principles of assertiveness, i.e., respecting yourself and others. Second, it will demonstrate for you that you really do have power, and that asserting this power in a win-win way could bring about different results.

Asserting Yourself with the Bully: What to Expect

When you finally have the courage to confront the bully, expect the bully to respond with one of the following three tactics: denial, counter-attack or victimhood. The bully does this in order to avoid taking responsibility for what you are trying to say. Remember, the bully cannot be "reasoned" with. They are out to win at any cost; they are not wired for win-win (and this is not your fault).

1. Denial

The bully will try and deny your "common sense" claim in order to gain back their control:

- Trivialization: "You're making a mountain out of a mole hill..." or "Get a grip, this is not even worth talking about..."

- Fresh Start Tactic: "I don't know why you're so intent on dwelling on the past" or "Look, what's past is past. I'll overlook your behavior and we'll start afresh." This is an abdication of responsibility by the bully and an attempt to divert and distract attention by using false conciliation.

2. Counter-Attack

- Right after the denial, the bully responds with aggressive counter-criticism or counter-allegation, based on distortion or fabrication:

- Lying, deception, duplicity, hypocrisy and blame.

- The purpose is to avoid answering the question and thus avoid accepting responsibility for the bullying behavior.

3. Victimhood

In the unlikely event of denial and counter-attack being insufficient, the bully plays the victim by manipulating through guilt:

- Self-pity, pretending indignation, acting "devastated".

- Claiming to be "deeply offended" and maintaining that he is the one being bullied.

What can you do?

1. Know, and really internalize, that the bully very rarely will look for a win-win solution. Do not expect one.

2. The bully will never say "sorry" or show you compassion or empathy (which is exactly what you are hoping for in order to feel better).

3. Remind yourself that, although you cannot seem to "get through" to the bully, you are no less of a person, and that most of these cases, people like yourself feel exactly the same.

PS: Just knowing this is a small measure of hope, and hopefully you will begin to see that rationalizing with a bully will never come to pass. Start putting your energy on getting stronger internally, as opposed to hoping for the bully to "come around".

Preparing to Confront

As you think about confronting the bully, remind yourself about the difference in your values and hers. Don't fool yourself into thinking that she will listen to reason, that "if you explain how you feel", she will come to see the "error of her ways". You may be all about mutual respect and getting along, but she values control and power.

Considering How to Approach the Bully

Most targets do not want to "take it anymore", and rightly so. Most targets also feel that by saying something, they themselves will gain back some measure of power they feel they have lost.

Consider saying something if:

1. You realize the fact that you were targeted to be bullied is not your fault. There is never an excuse for such win-lose behavior.

2. You truly do not expect the bully to change. Hoping so will actually decrease your power.

3. You can say something with confidence and then walk away; not engaging in dialogue with expectations of "realizations" and "negotiations".

By saying something to the bully you may:

1. Set a boundary to let the bully know their bullying tactics are not appropriate and you will not tolerate them.

2. Feel empowered and more confident, because it is you that has set the boundary.

You can say it in two ways:
1. In person (write it out first, practice, then go for it)
2. In writing

Here's an example:

A. "Since _____": (state when the behavior began).

B. "You have chosen to conduct behavior towards me that is _____": (list two-three behaviors that are specific and clear such as: threatening, unacceptable, inexcusable, intimidating, condescending).

C. "Specifically you have _____": (list two-three things they have done specifically to you).

D. Be brief and to the point listing the "what". "What you have done has no validity and I believe you do this in order to attempt to gain control." (You are telling them you know).

E. "Your behavior _____": (tell the impact on you, for example: prevents me from completing my work, causes me to not be informed and therefore not contribute properly).

F. "I am asking you to stop behaving this way _____ (list the behaviors again) towards me, effective immediately. A copy of this letter will remain on file. I will take further action if you do not comply with my request. Sincerely, (your name)."

Your main points should focus on the behavior that is a problem for you, its effects (briefly), and what you want done about it. You don't need to blame the bully, but *don't* make excuses for her (such as "I know you're under a lot of pressure..."). Just stick to the problem-effects-request formula.

> Just stick to the problem-effects-request formula.

When you're ready to confront the bully, try to relax as much as you can. But what if you're nervous? That's okay. Most people would be nervous in this situation. You can still handle it. Just take three deep breaths and continue saying to yourself, "Relax...I have the right to have my needs met, not at the expense of myself or others - it will be okay - the sun will still rise tomorrow."

Rehearsing your main points will help relax you, because it will give you some structure to follow during the conversation.

Rehearsing will also keep you on track, to actually say what you need to say. Going into the discussion without having your main points in mind may lead to "soft pedalling", over-explaining or complete avoidance of the issue on your part.

Choose an issue. Should you just pick bullying in general as the problem? Or should you pick a specific incident? That depends. If the person is likely to completely deny bullying you and there is a significant incident you can record, it's probably better to use that. If the bullying consists of a pattern of trivial incidents, though, you may want to simply identify bullying as the problem and be prepared to record several examples of the behavior.

You can write your main points like this:

The problem is: _____

Effects on me: _____

I request that: _____

Example:
"I'm tired of you making fun of me in front of others; for example, when you called me 'Simple Simon'. This embarrasses me. I'd like you to stop."

Confronting the Bully Is HARD

Have you ever been frustrated because the bully at work does not hear you? Have you found yourself working up the courage to say something, only to be ignored, dismissed, or handled? Do you find yourself feeling confused and once again going over in your mind "how to say it" so that the bully at work will hear you?

Why the bully at work appears not to hear you – 2 reasons:

1. The bully at work is into being in control – always. It is an addiction. They do not look to share and care. If you say black, they look to see white; all in an effort to avoid connecting with you. If we can truly understand the bully's need for control, we will also realize most bullies do not seek to "understand" others.

2. The second reason is we are not easily understandable. Many times we will tend to over-explain, apologize, back-track, or give up, in order to curb rejection from the bully at work. Clarity, confidence, and command of what you are saying is key to avoid any possible confusion and not give the bully at work an "out" to respecting your needs.

There are four basic principles to keep in mind when confronting a bully. The acronym HARD will help you remember them.

- **Honest.** Always be honest. You'll feel so much better about how you handled yourself. Besides, it's so much easier than trying constantly to come up with "the right thing to say." This doesn't mean you have to bare your soul. Just make sure that whatever you do share is completely honest and candid. Just be yourself.

- **Agreeable.** Agree where you can to demonstrate that you want to cooperatively resolve the problem. Never agree to anything you don't believe. For example, if the bully should sneer at you and say "Look at you – you're shaking in your boots!", you can agree that yes, you're nervous, but that it's still important to you to work it out.

Never defend yourself. It will only put you in a weakened position, making the conversation about your shortcomings instead of the real issue at hand, which is the bullying. Agreeing with the person appropriately basically takes all the air out of the bully's balloon when he tries to blame you.

Don't argue. The person may bring up points he knows are sensitive to you, just to "get your goat". or put you in a defensive position and get you arguing. Don't fall for it.

Example:

Bully: "What do you expect? You're always late. You hold everyone up."

You (defensive) "That's only because my carpool is late sometimes. I've tried taking the bus but that's even worse." (The two of you will now argue about the tardiness issue.)

You (agreeable): "Yes, I have been late a few times. And we can talk about that another time. But right now the issue is your bullying."

- **Respectful.** Always treat yourself and the other person with respect. If the person is disrespectful to you, you can say "Don't speak to me like that, please." If it continues, you can end the discussion. "I want to resolve this problem, but I can see you aren't willing to treat me with respect."

Part of having respect for yourself and others is taking personal responsibility. Use "I" statements instead of "you" statements when possible. Instead of saying what the bully should do, say what you want. For instance,

167

say "I need your cooperation..." rather than "You need to stop..."

> Instead of saying what the bully should do, say what *you* want.

Don't grovel or flatter, to ingratiate yourself with the bully. The first is disrespectful (to yourself), the second is dishonest, and they are both ineffective. This will only remind the bully that he has power over you.

- **Direct.** Be direct. Speak simply. Clearly state what you want. It's easy to go off track when you're nervous and intimidated. The bully may also bring up irrelevant issues to muddy the waters, but try and keep focused on your main points. If things get off track, bring them back to the issue. Try to elicit the person's specific agreement to do what you want (such as to stop teasing you). If he's evasive, keep going back to the same point. "I understand that. So, you're agreeing to stop teasing me, right?"

How to Talk to the Bully: A Classy, Crucial Conversation That Counts

Have you ever wondered how to say what you need to say to the bully... not at the expense of the bully or yourself?

Classy: Respectful, win-win, seeking the best for all.

Crucial: A needed conversation to move an issue forward for what's "best" for the company.

Conversation: A dialogue where both people are engaged and exchanging ideas and information.

Counts: Be sure that the conversation ends with a resolution or shared agreement.

Keys for a classy crucial conversation:

1. In order to have more control, the target should decide when the conversation will take place. Do not react to when the bully attacks you; decide when you are ready to converse in order to get the best outcome.

2. As a target, the bully is hoping you do not have the strength to stand up for yourself. She feels better when you are down.

3. By having a classy crucial conversation you will be starting to set stronger boundaries, which will protect you and help to avoid future conflicts.

How to proceed:

1. Clearly define what the situation is - something you wished was different; for example, a behavior or a circumstance.

2. What would you like to see happen instead of the stated situation above?

3. Use the Classy Crucial Conversation Planner to assist you.

Using the Classy Crucial Conversation Planner:

1. Start with a classy statement to show your good will, as opposed to a demand. Example: "My desire is to

have a win-win in the office and to support you and our customers as best as I can."

2. Add another classy statement in the form of a question: "Can I share something with you?" (the invitation).

3. The conversation:

"*I notice when…*you comment at meetings, you often swear." (Behavioral facts as you see them);

"*I feel/think…*shocked and ashamed" or "*It…*puts me in an awkward position." (The impact of how it affects you personally - how it made you think/feel or what it has caused you);

"*I appreciate…*you are under a lot of stress." (Acknowledge their position);

"*However, in the future I would like:* if you would stop using swear words at meetings." (a request);

Then state: "*Would you be willing to do this? Yes or No.*" (Stay until you receive an answer!)

- If yes – confirm agreement: "Just so I'm clear, our agreement is…"
- If later the agreement is broken: "I thought our agreement was…"
- If no – Ask "Why?" You may need more information, e.g., maybe they have a good reason or a different understanding.

Asking for an agreement helps close the request and the target then knows where she stands. Many targets think that simply expressing their hurt feelings and disappointment to the bully will solve the problem. This leaves the power in the bully's hands. Keep leading the conversation request by requiring accountability with a question – yes or no.

After the Confrontation

It would indeed be a miracle if confronting the bully would suddenly make her a delightful person. That isn't likely to happen. Rarely will a bully apologize on the spot, so don't hold out for this. They may reflect later, realize that you're not such an easy target after all, and stop bullying you.

Make a detailed log entry of your conversation with her, including any agreements that were made. Hope that she will keep her word, but take it with a grain of salt.

4. Severe Bullying

Severe bullying is when you're being pummelled. Maybe you're so totally overwhelmed by the bullying that you simply cannot "pull it together" enough to defend yourself. Or else, despite your assertive responses, the bully is out of control, potentially dangerous.

To handle severe bullying, you'll require all of the skills and tools needed for minor and moderate-level bullying, and more. This type of bullying requires an intervention of policy and company rules that are enforced in order to keep the bully in line, and to protect you. You may need to get outside help. You might also be facing a decision about whether to stay in your job or leave.

> **Skills and Tools to Handle Severe Bullying:**
> - Acknowledge the bullying.
> - Bully-proof yourself.
> - Protect yourself.
> - Manage your stress level.
> - Build your self-esteem.
> - Empower yourself.
> - Enlist support.
> - Assert yourself with the bully.
> - Decide whether to get help in your organization.

Deciding Whether or Not to Get Help in Your Organization

This is more of a realization than a decision. Unless you're confident you can handle the situation by applying the skills you have learned, you should get help. That is, if help is available. Is it feasible to go to your supervisor or to approach Human Resources for their intervention? Will doing so help resolve the problem so that you can continue in your job? Will it have no effect, or even make matters worse? Do you have a concern about confidentiality? Only you know your specific work situation in order to make this judgment. Naturally, you'll want the support and advice from your support team to help you gauge the pros and cons of asking for help.

I would say, though, that if you are confident that discussing the matter with, say, your supervisor or Human Resources would not backfire on you in any way, then by all means talk to them.

Deciding Whether to Stay or Go

If your job is very important to you, deciding whether to go or stay can be a heart-wrenching decision. After all, through no fault of your own, you may be forced to give up something you value very much. If, on the other hand, the job and organization aren't as important to you, you might be only too glad to leave.

5. Prepare to Leave, Even If You Don't

One of the most empowering things you can do for yourself when you're being bullied at work is to create choices for yourself. Put yourself in a position so that you can leave - or stay. The point is that you want to be able to make the choice yourself.

What Are You Afraid Of?

First, you need to take a good, honest look at your fears and vulnerabilities. Are you walking around with a sense of dread and uncertainty? Do worries constantly sneak up on you, despite your best efforts to keep your mind off them? Maybe it's more serious and you're suffering episodes of panic. Anxiety is normal when you're going through uncertain times. But trying to keep your fears out of your conscious thinking doesn't make them go away; it only drives them into the shadows. There, they can slowly eat away at you while you do nothing to stop it. Why not invite the bogeyman to come out of the closet, where you can have a good look at him and size him up in the light of day instead?

Assignment: Preparing to Leave

In this assignment, you will flush out your fears, identify factors that help and hinder you from leaving your work situation, and begin an action plan to correct deficits.

- Find a blank page in your journal and write the heading "Fears." Ask yourself, "What are my very biggest fears at the moment?" and consider this for several minutes. Then jot down a few words to represent your thoughts, such as "losing my job." Probe each fear to uncover a deeper, more basic fear underneath it. For example, losing your job might not bother you if you had another one lined up, so you might write "out of work.....money trouble" and "I'd feel like a failure."

- Next, write the heading "Exit Strategy" and, under that "Assets and Potential Obstacles." What specific skills, knowledge and experience do you have that will help you get your next job? What deficits might you have, such as no resume and not enough money saved? Write down the assets and potential obstacles that come to mind. There is no need for an exhaustive list. It's better to focus on a few important ones.

- Then write "Actions I Will Take." Review each potential obstacle. What you can do about them? Jot down tangible actions that you can take to address each obstacle.

Example:

My Fears
Having to quit job – money trouble – where do I fit in?
Being fired – feel like a failure.
New job – what if I fail – bullies there?

Exit Strategy

Assets	Potential Obstacles
Job:	
7 years experience	No degree
Can work flexible hours	Why I left current job?
Longevity in current job	Outdated resume
Good performance reviews	Not good in interviews
Get along well with others	

> Other: Not enough savings
>   Don't know where to start
>
> **Actions I Will Take**
> - No degree – Not huge obstacle. Take courses to update my technical skills.
> - How to explain why I left current job – Explore further opportunity, attach a performance review.
> - Outdated resume - Ask Sandy to help update.
> - Not good at interviews - Get book, ask Sandy to help.
> - Not enough savings - Save 3 months more pay. Go on a budget – simplify!
> - Don't know where to start - Make list of contacts: friends, people at church, volunteer center - Start looking at job listings - Research companies.

Great Decision Making

A great decision-making process should be structured. Having structure helps ensure that you don't leave out any important actions. It can also be extremely comforting in times of doubt and uncertainty. Your best decisions are those made using a structured process and your instincts; in other words, engaging both your head and your heart.

Before you reach the point where you're seriously contemplating leaving your job, you will probably have considered other ways of handling the problem. Those are the options you identified back in Chapter 7, **Empower Yourself**, and wrote in your journal. Remember the three steps in making a decision:

- Identify your options.

- Evaluate the options.

- Choose an option.

You've already stated the problem and identified possible solutions. Now it's time to evaluate your options and decide what you want to do. If you have thought of any others since you identified your options, go ahead and add them to the list.

Assignment: Decision-Making Step #2 - Evaluating Your Options

- Go to the "Step 2 – Evaluate Options" page in your journal.
- Take each option one at a time and consider its pros and cons, based on the information you have at this time. Write them down. Underline the advantages and disadvantages of particular importance to you. If there are obstacles attached to a certain option, make a note. For instance, obstacles associated with the option of looking for a new job might be "outdated resume" and "not enough savings."
- Your options and their pros and cons might seem very obvious to you, so it is vital to talk over your alternatives with your support team. Their objectivity and distance from the situation may steer you to consider an idea that you otherwise might throw out, thinking that "it is no use."

Example:
Statement of Problem:

Who: Paul Harwood

What/How Often: Makes fun of me in front of others by pre-calling poor job performance on my part; not giving me specific deadlines and then saying I was late turning in my project. Each time I've been in contact this past week, an incident such as above has occurred.

The Effects: This is causing me insomnia; and it is hard to concentrate on my job. I also feel left out and demoralized, and am beginning to doubt my own abilities.

Step #1: Identify Your Options
1. Ignore him.
2. Avoid him.
3. Try harder to get along with him.
4. Talk to him – what is the problem?.
5. Talk to him – ask him to lay off.
6. Threaten to report him.
7. Talk to supervisor.
8. Talk to HR – get advice.
9. Talk to HR – report him.
10. Write note to Paul – ask him to lay off.
11. Ask for transfer out of Warehouse.
12. Campaign – assert myself at every encounter.
13. Look for another job.
14. Take legal action against company.

Step #2: Evaluate Your Options

Pros:	Cons:
1. Ignore	None; things will just get worse.
2. Avoid	Don't have to deal with it – we work too closely.
3. Get along	None; he gets worse when I try.
4. Talk about problem?	Might work it out. Or, he might get worse. He might reject me.
5. Lay off	He might cooperate. Or he might get worse.
6. Threaten	He might stop, might call my bluff or force me to follow through with it. Do I want to?
7. Talk to supervisor.	Might be able to help. He already sees the bullying. I may be seen as a complainer.
8. HR advice	Suggestions? Do something – confidential? I may be seen as a complainer or troublemaker.
9. HR report	Discipline Paul, fire him – things might blow up! Transfer him, transfer me. Paul might wage war.

177

Pros:	Cons:
10. Write Paul	None; would make things worse.
11. Transfer	No more Paul! Where to? Lose seniority? Stress! New job? Commute, etc. Note: Update resume.
12. Assert myself	Might end problem. Stressful – health? Self-esteem. Note: Need support, training (counselor? training through work?)
13. New job	No more Paul, fresh start. Job? Pay? Commute? How long out of work? Note: Update resume, finish certification.

Assignment: Decision-Making Step #3 - Choose an Option

Once you feel you know all of your options, and have evaluated each of them honestly and objectively, you're ready to decide what action you want to take. Write down your option and include any action items you'll need to address in order to accomplish the option. Remember: Not choosing an option means you will still be in the same place you are at now.

Example:
Step #3: Choose Option (Identify action steps to address any obstacles).

1st choice: Launch campaign to assert myself with Paul. Will need help sticking with this? Look into assertiveness training through company, other assertiveness and self-esteem resources and/or counselling.

2nd choice: Transfer to other department. Do if #1 option doesn't work. Give it 3 months. Meanwhile, update resume and start looking at postings.

The previous example is about a decision to leave the job but remain at the organization. Maybe staying with your organization or even at your job is your preferred choice. If so, I truly hope it will work out for you. It's always good to have insurance, though. Being in a position to be able to leave your job or organization if you should decide to is just insurance in case things don't work out. Bolstering your situation and increasing your options shifts the power to you, which may actually enable you to be more effective in your current situation.

As I said earlier in this book, no one would willingly sign up to be bullied. But it happens. Before moving on with your life, take a little time to take stock of where you are and to replenish your energy.

If you feel a bit jittery about being assertive or even making a new start, that's okay. This feeling will go away in time in your new, friendlier environment. Perhaps you're feeling a little unsure of yourself. Again, that's natural. The bullying experience was a direct assault on your self-esteem. And, while I hope through all of this you have been able to actually increase your feelings of self-esteem and confidence, let's face it: the wounds are still fresh. So be patient with yourself. Before long, the ordeal will be a mere memory.

Continue working on your assertiveness skills. Remember: practice, practice, practice! Continue building your self-esteem. Empower yourself by cherishing and ever increasing your level of wellness. Honour your own values, always. Be proud of yourself for coming through this challenging experience.

> May today mark the beginning of many new joys and accomplishments...and a continuation of all the good things that you have already achieved.

CHAPTER 9

The Top 21 Tips

Overview

1. Ask Yourself: Are You Watering Seeds or Weeds?
2. "Fair" and "Unfair" Conversations: Know the Difference for Increased Power
3. What Do You Do with Your Feelings?
4. How Anger and Frustration Are Expressed: Heavy Control
5. How Anger and Frustration Are Expressed: Passive Control
6. What Will You Do with Your Anger and Frustration?
7. Say What You Mean and Mean What You Say
8. Responding to Discounting
9. Avoiding the Issue: Keeping You Powerless
10. Sarcasm—It's NOT Funny
11. Mind Reading
12. Being Interrupted
13. Mirroring
14. Making Requests
15. Respond with "I Understand" or "I See"
16. Gunny-Sacking
17. Cold Shoulder Treatment
18. Acting Like You've Made an Unreasonable Request
19. What to Do When the Bully Attacks You with Untrue Accusations
20. Short, Simple Come-Backs to Use with Bullies
21. How to Change Workplace Bullying: You Really Can Have Something Better!

1. Ask Yourself: Are You Watering Seeds or Weeds?

Many times, our attention is spent on "what to do about the bullying" and we cannot seem to think of anything else until this problem is not only handled, but healed. Why not choose to focus your attention on the wonderful seeds you've planted over your lifetime - good friends, good family, caring co-workers, even the pleasant waitress who always manages to give you a warm smile when you come in? The positivity and encouragement from these people is there for you.

- Notice what is already there.

- Water these "seeds" in order to reinforce your relations and weave a solid network of support.

- Stop watering the "weeds" - dwelling, worrying, wondering about the bully in your life. Try doing this for one hour, one day, one week...

> **Empowerment Tip**
>
> What can we do to water the seeds, and create a great supportive relationship?
>
> Here are three essential elements that create positive rapport:
>
> 1. Shared attention: When two people attend to what each other says and does. This generates mutual interest, which in turn creates shared feelings.
>
> 2. Mutual empathy: Both people experience being "experienced". You sense the other person's desire to tune into your needs and feelings.

> 3. Alignment of verbal and non-verbal communication: Does the body language match what the person is saying? Look for an open body position (versus crossed arms), and eye contact (versus avoidance). In alignment, people express themselves freely and are comfortable with silence.

There are good positive seeds already growing in your backyard, just waiting for you! Know that watering the "seeds" can help you become bully free from the "weeds"!

2. "Fair" and "Unfair" Conversations: Know the Difference for Increased Power

Have you ever felt bewildered right in the middle of a conversation, wondering to yourself "What on earth is happening here?" or "I want to work this out in a fair way, but I feel the other person is acting unfairly"?

If the other person is acting out unfairly, then you'll want to bully-proof yourself. Here's how you can tell what is fair and unfair in terms of a conversation:

1. Facial expression
Fair Conversation: Responsive and interested
Unfair Conversation: Closed and passive

2. Focus
Fair Conversation: Concentrates on your issue and is present (paying attention)
Unfair Conversation: Over-generalizations; dumps many issues at once in order to deflect and defend

3. Rapport
Fair Conversation: Shared purpose, empathetic
Unfair Conversation: One-way and no direct response/
                       feedback

4. How information is handled
Fair Conversation: Realistic and authentic
Unfair Conversation: Distorted and lies

5. Responsibility to successful conclusion
Fair Conversation: Willing to resolve and change
Unfair Conversation: Denial, justifications and avoiding

> ### Empowerment Tip
> Knowing what an unfair conversation looks like will help you to realize that you are not crazy when you meet up with a bully. Keeping a realistic perspective will help you to distance yourself from being drawn into the bully's power.

3. What Do You Do with Your Feelings?

Have you ever experienced a situation where you felt:

- **Misunderstood** – You explain your point of view and someone goes on a completely different tangent from what you are saying. You feel: Invalidated.

- **Judged** – You drive to a meeting and a fellow colleague comments on how your car "needs a bit of work". You take this as a personal attack; why should the state of your car matter? You feel: Hurt.

- **Disrespected** – You organize a meeting, set the time and place, and make all the arrangements and detailed planning. At the last minute, your boss decides not to go "because he can". You feel: Unsupported and shunned.

- **Not affirmed or acknowledged** – You are the one who came early and stayed late each day to complete a rush project; in fact, you got it done under budget and on time. Your boss does not even thank you and actually takes the credit! You feel: Angry and overlooked.

Did you know that these four types of situations are what cause most of us to experience some emotional resistance to what is going on? What do you do with these feelings?

Do you:

1. Bottle them up so tightly that you stop feeling altogether?
    - This is okay to survive, but not to ultimately thrive.
    - We end up by going numb.
    - We block out the fear, anger, frustration and pain.
    - And we end up blocking out the good feelings of pleasure, joy and love as well.

2. Leak out your frustration in destructive ways?
    - This is common for those who want to "protect" our co-workers, friends and family from our problems.
    - We act as if "everything is okay" and even put on a happy face, but….
    - All is takes is for the TV to be too loud or the garbage to be overflowing in the staff room for us to blow up and display bitter or sarcastic behavior.
    - We may even pick a fight to channel our frustrations.

> **Empowerment Tip**
>
> Knowing what you do with your feelings (awareness) is important in order for you to:
> 1. Identify how you come across to others and
> 2. Understand how you physically, mentally, emotionally and spiritually handle your emotions to determine 'who you want to be'.

4. How Anger and Frustration Are Expressed: Heavy Control

How is your anger and frustration expressed? Most of us in a professional environment try to show that "it doesn't matter", and that we can "handle it". Eventually that wears off and our emotions leak out aggressively (directly) or passive-aggressively (indirectly) or not at all (passively), and we internalize everything into our bodies. What is underlying everything is anger. Did you know that anger is a secondary emotion? What's really beneath anger? Fear and pain.

Why the challenge?

- Most of us were taught to "suck it up" and not cry, and to "build a bridge and get over it", thereby avoiding the concept of feeling pain.

- We may have been taught that being angry is dangerous or wrong, so we attempt to dispense of the anger as soon as possible by suppressing it.

- Some of us are confused and we quickly stuff or project our feelings. We are then left with a suppression of pain and fear, but also with a suppression of joy, love, tenderness, aliveness – we stop feeling everything altogether.

Heavy control – what is it?

Heavy control is using a demanding tone and harsh words – you feel like you were hit by a truck when you experience them.

Here are some ways it occurs:

1. **Name calling:** "You're so stupid."
2. **Mind reading:** "You wouldn't do that."
3. **Blaming:** "We wouldn't be in this predicament if you…"
4. **Accusing:** "You just hung around like a lost puppy."
5. **Threatening:** "You'd better fix this or else you're fired."
6. **Demanding:** "Just get out of here."
7. **Ordering:** "Don't do this until you do that."
8. **Criticizing:** "That way won't get you anywhere. Why don't you…?"
9. **Taunting:** "Your department is never wrong; you're all perfect, aren't you?"
10. **Sarcasm:** "Well, look who's finally graced us with her presence."

> **Empowerment Tip**
>
> Awareness is empowerment. Recognize heavy control for what is really is in order to be Bully Free At Work.

5. How Anger and Frustration Are Expressed: Passive Control

What is passive control?

It is a sneaky subtlety that is indirect and "behind the scenes", which as an end result still delivers a measure of control over another. The approach seems innocent, yet it stings; leaving the target feeling confused, hurt and angry.

Here are some ways that passive control plays out:

1. **Pseudo-questioning:** "Will you tell me what's so wrong with wanting to make sure we have all this work done?"

2. **Martyr:** "It doesn't matter. I'll manage somehow; I always do."

3. **Excuses:** "If I was feeling better, I'd be out there too."

4. **Whining:** "You can't seem to get things in order, can you?"

5. **Complaining:** "If it weren't for me, nothing would happen around here."

Other situations:

1. You go to a meeting, only to find out everyone else was notified that it started half an hour earlier. You were not told, leaving you arriving late and looking unprofessional. Not telling you is passive control.

2. You are out for lunch with your team, and your boss pays for everyone's lunch except yours. Your boss continues on as if nothing happened.

3. You need something from your boss and he keeps stalling, saying "I'll do it when I have time"; yet a company deadline is missed, leaving you holding the ball.

4. Ignoring – You try to address an issue directly, and your boss does not even acknowledge what you've said. She either does not respond, or changes the topic altogether.

5. Laughing or joking when you are trying to address a serious issue.

> **Empowerment Tip**
>
> Remember: Frustration occurs when someone does not receive, or hear, our anger and concern. Bullies do not care about reaching out to understand you.

6. What Will You Do with Your Anger and Frustration?

When a target has faced an injustice such as being bullied at work, many times the person wants to think of ways to "get back" at the bully and maintain a sense of justice. This thought process is one that often occurs in an attempt to deal with one's anger and frustration. It makes sense to "fight for justice", doesn't it?

> **Empowerment Tip**
>
> Consider this: We live in a system of "law" rather than "justice". Justice can be harder to achieve. Here are some things to consider if you feel the anger and frustration of being bullied and you are not sure what to do with these emotions:
>
> 1. Remember, bullying often occurs to kind, competent, considerate people. Don't get caught up in "What did I do to cause this? How can I change so the bully does not target me?" stage. Instead move to the "I am being bullied and I will now take steps to protect myself" stage.
>
> 2. Notice if you are feeling angry, frustrated or hurt. It is time to channel these feelings so they do not take a toll on your body, mind and well-being.

3. Know that if anyone is angry, frustrated or hurt over a period of time, their body *will* suffer. Make every attempt to move the energy through your body and resist the temptation to sit and analyze the situation time after time. Here are some tips for moving your energy:

    - Schedule time each day to exercise or get your heart rate up. If you are not engaged in an exercise routine right now, then consider kneeling in front of a bunch of pillows and hitting the pillows with both of your arms, yelling each time you hit the pillows. Do this for a total of one minute - give it everything you've got! This will give your body a chance to rid the 'negative energy' from your body and you will be surprised at how much better you will feel. The benefits of moving this energy out of your body, especially when you're experiencing the stress of bullying, will help prevent further health complications. Seriously, try it!

    - Journal. Try one page and just write until you are done. Then within a day, throw the paper out as a symbol of "moving on".

    Make a commitment to deal with your anger and frustration. Don't hope that it will just go away, or not creep up on you later in life. The commitment to yourself is key in terms of building enough energy to fight back, go for justice and build your life back.

7. Say What You Mean and Mean What You Say

If people could only say what they want, and want what they say. When dealing with workplace bullies, communication in the workplace is fraught with anemic requests and feeble declarations. People "beat around the bush", dancing from foot to foot as they ask for something.

Life would be so much simpler and richer if we could just say what we want and want what we say. This is one time when it's okay to feel entitled. There are handsome rewards for putting our wishes out there. Making our needs clearly known will enable us to enjoy freedom and self respect. Deciding to be clear on your needs at work is the first step to creating communication in the workplace that is solid and synergistic; and furthermore, you will create a necessary boundary against workplace bullies, showing them that you do have a voice.

There is a reason for these garbled messages. Targets - in fact, most people - are afraid to ask for what they want. Their internal self-talk goes something like this: "If I ask for what I want, and the other person denies me, then I'd prefer to sugar coat my request in order to feel less rejection." This fear of rejection is the motivator for the target and a godsend for workplace bullies.

1. It is painful to feel rejection. Most of us will go out of our way to avoid it.

2. People will say No to us. If we live our lives to secure a Yes every time we ask for something, we will cripple our ability to realize our desires.

3. In addition to shortchanging ourselves, we confuse our colleagues and live in quiet frustration.

4. The problem is confusing the rejection of one's ideas or requests with rejection of themselves.

Empowerment Tip

1. Understand that not being direct and clear may impact your productivity. Roundabout requests are often phrased as a question that puts the listener in

191

the driver's seat, such as asking "What are you doing this afternoon?" when the person really wants to say, "I'd like you to join me for coffee". The belief is that this way the rejection will be muted if the other person refuses to oblige.

2. Write out your request before you present it so that it is clear in your own mind. It is much harder for you to think clearly when your cognitions are couched in an overlay of emotion. If it is too hard to speak your truth directly to another, present the written request to the person concerned.

3. Know that you have a right and responsibility to speak your truth and make your wishes known to your co-workers as you communicate at work.

4. If asking for what you need is a nagging problem affecting all aspects of your life, then assertiveness training and coaching is a good idea to explore.

8. Responding to Discounting

Discounting is a form of abuse. It occurs when:

- Someone with authority over you makes a false statement, and insists that it is true;

- Someone uses back-handed humor or put downs in order to "put you in a lower position";

- Someone uses rudeness, ignoring, or verbal and non-verbal messages where you feel much "less than" as a result.

It goes something like this:

1. You are hurt by one of the behaviors above;

2. You respond by saying: "That's not true!" or "That wasn't very kind of you", etc.;

3. Their response is: "You are jumping to conclusions!" or "I don't know what you mean; you're over-reacting."

4. You feel even worse...

Keys to effectiveness:

1. Don't try to understand how someone could say this to you. You may never really know and bottom line - it does not have much to do with you.

2. Don't try to get them to understand that "you don't jump to conclusions...", etc. They are not interested in your enlightenment; they want to hold on to their views for their own protection.

> ### Empowerment Tip
>
> Respond with a clear direct statement such as:
> 1. "Stop."
> 2. "I don't want to hear this from you."
> 3. "I'm out."
>
> Remember: the bully does not want to take any responsibility for his actions. By being direct without hesitation, you show the bully that you do not share the same beliefs and you maintain your boundary (and protection) of control.
>
> Remember - you have the right to protect yourself from any abusive situation.

193

9. Avoiding the Issue: Keeping You Powerless

What happens:

1. You gain the confidence to say something to the bully, or respond to an accusation she made.

2. The bully replies with a statement that is unrelated to what you just said (changing the subject).

Here's how it works:

By changing the subject and using a counter-accusation such as blaming (you) or diverting (you) altogether, the bully acts as if she owns the conversation. This leaves you as the only flexible and giving person, and leaves her as "in control" by not working with you.

Here's how you feel:

1. Disconnected and unsupported – you are "putting yourself out there", only to encounter a closed door from the bully. By not being acknowledged by her, you feel unimportant, dishonoured and devalued.

2. Perplexed: You cannot believe the insensitivity of the bully in that she are not engaging with you, hearing you out or acknowledging you and your feelings about the situation.

Remember:

The tendency for the target is to spend energy analyzing their own behavior, which will only result in self doubt and wondering, "If I was (more clear), then would the bully acknowledge and hear me?" No! The bully has decided not to acknowledge you as a way of taking your power away.

> **Empowerment Tip**
>
> What you can do:
>
> 1. Recognize avoidance tactics, such as changing the subject or non-acknowledgement of what you are saying, as a losing proposition for resolution.
>
> 2. You can re-enter the conversation by repeating your phrase clearly and continually (broken record technique) as a stand off position to the bully.

P.S. You are no less of a person if you cannot get through to a bully.

10. Sarcasm – It's *Not* Funny

What happens:

You feel hurt about a meaningful issue and you want to resolve this with the bully. You may not even say anything directly, but whatever you do, you can't quite put your finger on what's happening. There appears to be a joke, but you don't feel like laughing.

Sarcasm:

Remarks that are expressed that have an opposite affect on you. They are expressed as a joke, but the target feels hurt. For example, you arrive at work and you look particularly nice today. The bully says, "Oh, the Queen has arrived." Hmm… you don't feel much like a queen after hearing that comment.

Here's how you feel:

Everyone seems to be laughing and you are left wondering what happened, because you don't feel like laughing. Instead, you feel disjoined, confused and left out.

What's happening:

This creative aggression technique – sarcasm – is confusing, leaving you bewildered and powerless. It is so subtle, many do not recognize its damning effects. The bully feels powerful while the target feels confused.

> ### Empowerment Tip
>
> What you can do:
>
> 1. Know that if you do not feel like laughing, you are probably correct in your feelings. Trust your feelings.
> 2. Say "That sounds like a put down to me", and leave the issue/situation. This sets a boundary between you and the bully.
> 3. When you set the boundary, you set the power differential.

P.S. When we have clear boundaries, we know where the bully stops and where we start. Where and when will you choose your boundary to stop the bully?

11. Mind Reading

What happens:

Mind reading occurs when the bully is "psychoanalyzing" and jumping to conclusions about what you think. He makes a statement about what you are apparently thinking, before you have a chance to say or share your truth.

For example:

Bully: "You've probably already decided to leave early today. Everyone always does when the going gets tough."

Target: Was actually planning to stay and work late, even though he or she had other plans.

Mind reading is psychoanalyzing and jumping to conclusions. It is not giving you the chance and room to say what is true for you. The conversation starts off with an assumption. If the bully mindreads and then adds a condescending tone of voice with some force, the target has to be careful and not get caught in the bully's web.
Remember, the bully wants to gain control by taking your power. Your power is your power. Protect your power by "checking in" to see if this is true for you, rather than second guessing yourself. You are not crazy!

Empowerment Tip

What you can do:

If a bully makes a statement, stop and pause to ask "Is this true for me?". Check in with yourself to see if the statement makes sense to you. If it does not represent your reality, you have two choices:

1. State what is true for you, for example "Actually, that isn't true; I was planning to stay and work late".
2. Ignore the bully, especially if you feel they are being so unreasonable that your voice would not be heard.

Note: In order for you to feel good about your actions, do not simply walk away, but acknowledge the bully by looking them in the eye and then walk away quietly. Know that you are NOT at fault; the bully was attempting to pull you into a web.

12. Being Interrupted

What happens:

How do you feel when you are interrupted or you are cut off from your thoughts? For most people, the occasional "cut off" is mildly annoying. If it happens frequently however, being interrupted or cut off deliberately becomes alienating and hurtful; and you can feel misunderstood, dismissed and devalued.

You might ponder these questions:

- "Why am I being interrupted?"
- "What did I do?"
- "Did I say it clearly, properly, and with enough confidence?"
- "Am I important enough to be heard?"

First of all, remember: there is never an excuse for rudeness, dismissal, disrespect or any condescending behavior such as constant interrupting.

If you are being interrupted or cut off on a regular basis, either the person is:

1. Unaware or
2. Aware.

Bullies are aware.

Empowerment Tip

What you can do:
1. If someone is unaware that they are interrupting you:
   - Give the person the benefit of the doubt, and kindly but firmly say "Excuse me, I wasn't finished", and proceed to finish.

2. If someone is aware they are interrupting you:
   - Use the same technique;
   - And remember that the bully who is aware will likely push back. Be prepared and continue to stand your ground kindly and firmly.

Keys to Effectiveness:

1. Know that being interrupted shows insensitivity on the part of the other person – not a lack of worth about you.
2. Know that you have the right to jump back into the conversation with a kind but firm statement.
3. Know that being calm and confident shows power. It is the power that the bully wants. Keep it working for you.
4. Resist the temptation to wonder about your self-worth.

13. Mirroring

Repeat the exact words someone says when you disagree. This mirroring technique can keep both the speaker and the listener "centered" in a difficult conversation, as the attitude of the person doing the mirroring is to gain understanding of a different point of view. This shows strength and confidence: exactly what the bully does not know how to handle.

Empowerment Tip

A good way to repeat what someone says is, "What I hear you saying is…". State word for word what was said. Short sentences are best.

14. Make Requests

Make requests. It is often much more useful to make a request than to share your anger.

> **Empowerment Tip**
>
> If someone is not including you in an email exchange, then you could say: "I'd like to be included in your emails as I need to know when the meetings are." You then go on record as 'knowing' what the bully may be up to.

15. Respond with "I Understand" or "I See"

Respond with "I understand" or "I see". This phrase will support your goals when emotions are evident, and it does not commit you to the other person's demands. Use this as a bridge to find common ground to form compromises and agreements; or to simply hold off the bully.

> **Empowerment Tip**
>
> Less is more. Simply say "I see". That will be enough. Stop.

16. Gunny-Sacking

This occurs when the bully brings up more than one issue or complaint at a time. These issues or complaints about you may not necessarily be true. By "gunny-sacking" and dumping on you, you feel overwhelmed, cornered and thwarted. The bully's plan is to nail you down so you cannot get up.

> **Empowerment Tip**
>
> Don't get caught up in trying to respond to every request. Remove yourself from what is being said in order to avoid responding or reacting emotionally.

17. Cold-Shoulder Treatment

This occurs when the bully gives you the "silent treatment" by ignoring you, walking away from you or pouting. This can feel extremely confusing, as you cannot figure out what you've done to cause this. Remember the bully's behavior does not equal who you really are. Again, these strategies are confusing and hard to detect. They are irresponsible and dehumanizing.

> **Empowerment Tip**
>
> Pick your fights. If you must converse with the bully, use your physical presence and body language to make it obvious that you are there, and you are not to be ignored.

18. Acting Like You've Made an Unreasonable Request

This is a deflection technique to draw attention to the "unreasonableness" of your request rather than hearing your request. According to the bully, your request is made up of over-reactive emotional statements and defensiveness; the bully tries to turn the conversation to his needs rather than to make any attempt to hear you.

Awareness is step number one to self-empowerment, with an emphasis on "power". Know that when the bully uses these techniques, he or she can be disregarded.

> **Empowerment Tip**
>
> Remain calm, be silent and patient, then repeat your request again, exactly as you did the first time. By doing so, you are showing you are not endorsing the bully's unreasonable push back.

19. What to Do When the Bully Attacks You with Untrue Accusations

"How do I stop a 'bully boss' from attacking me with untrue accusations? He believes the customer over me. When I try and interrupt him, he puts me on hold."

Ask: "What does my boss want?"

1. The boss probably wants to be seen as competent and capable; in fact, most of us do.

2. Consider that it may be difficult for this boss to know exactly how to handle the customer's complaint. They may be wrestling with the concepts of "never make the customer wrong" and "any employee behavior is seen as a reflection on this boss personally". This boss may have trouble separating the customer's needs with supporting and leading employees.

3. This boss probably wants to heard out, without interruption; especially since they may have just had it out with a customer.

Ask: "What do I want?"

1. What do we want from our boss? Usually support, recognition and to be believed.

2. We want our boss to listen to us until we feel heard.

3. We want our boss to listen to the customer without compromising the morale of the staff.

What's really going on?

1. The boss is responsible for running the company and maintaining happy customers and staff.

2. The boss would be more apt to listen to an employee if he felt supported by being allowed to speak until he was finished (even if he is wrong and making false accusations).

3. The boss may be trying to maintain his own need to be seen as effective over getting to the truth of the matter (your view versus the customer's view).

Empowerment Tip

What You Can Do:

1. Allow your boss to finish his statements, especially if there is anger attached to them. Let the hot air out of the balloon first.

2. Remind yourself that by pushing back at that particular time, you will not likely win.

3. Choose to approach your boss after the dust settles and when your boss has time to hear you.

4. Have a "classy" crucial conversation that counts! (Taking the high road to where you want to lead the bully).

20. Short, Simple Come-Backs to Use with Bullies

You've mustered the courage to say something. You think, "I have finally stood up to the bully," and when you do, she has a harsh come-back. Are you prepared?

Be prepared – there will most likely be a come-back from most bullies when they are confronted. Remember, they do not care, and they are often not aware. Also remember, if they were operating from a secure base of high self esteem, they would usually naturally reach out to your statements with concern and compassion. Remember who you are dealing with.

You've said something...
There's a come-back...
Now it's your turn!

You can use this short simple approach with all office bullies.

> ### Empowerment Tip
>
> Here are three "Less Is More" short simple come-backs to help you deal with situations with bullies.
>
> 1. Bullies who talk on and on, pressuring you to agree with them. You feel you have to say something, but you don't want to give your power away by showing you agree. Less is More: Say "Interesting" or "Oh". This does not commit you!
>
> 2. Bullies who are rude with sarcasm, put downs or back-handed statements that are not necessarily direct, but harmfully subtle. You want to address it, so you say "That seems direct" or "That seems harsh" or "That seems like a put-down to me". The concept of using "That seems..." highlights your perception

> only, and it is enough of a diffusing comment to confuse the power plan of most bullies.
>
> 3. Sometimes we feel we have to have a come-back in order to be powerful. Be silent and just stare back with confidence. This is the position that "the come-back doesn't even deserve an acknowledgement".

21. How to Change Workplace Bullying: You Really Can Have Something Better!

People usually know what they *don't* want – we hear it in coffee shops, phone calls, at the water cooler, etc. Have you ever considered that too much time spent on what you don't want, with very little time actively spent on what you do want, might just create more of the same?

Principle #1: You Get What You Expect – What Are You Expecting?

It all started with driving into the downhill skiing parking lot with Jack and Ted. The parking lot was packed. I said, "Jack, you'd better park here. We'll never get a parking spot up front." Jack said, "We're going to the front – I'm expecting a spot." Guess what happened? Sure enough, there was a spot. I was humbled. I am a professional speaker and my job is to inspire others – alas, the teacher becomes the student!

I remember making a decision right at that moment: "Whenever I come skiing, I am going to expect a parking spot right at the front." Guess what happened? At the end of the season, I was 21 for 21! You got it – right in the front.

You can apply this principle in any situation, including bullying in the workplace. How does it work?

1. Be aware of what you do *not* want.

Example:	"I do not want to park far away."
Example:	"I do not want to be overlooked for my opinion by the workplace bully in the next staff meeting."

2. Replace what you don't want with what you *do* want instead.

Example:	"I want to park at the front."
More powerful:	"I will park at the front."
Example:	"I want to be able to share my opinion in the next staff meeting."
More powerful:	"I will be solicited for my opinion in the next staff meeting."

3. Create the belief – see it.

Example:	Picture yourself parking in the front.
Example:	Picture yourself sharing your opinion in the staff meeting, and being acknowledged for it.

Note:

- This cancels out your other (very active) mental picture of parking at the back – again; or being stonewalled by the workplace bully and not being asked your opinion in the staff meeting – again.

- We always have a mental picture of something. Which one will you choose?

- Yes, this may seem uncomfortable and perhaps difficult – try it anyway.

Why does this principle work?

When we expect something, we send off vibrations; and strangely enough, many times we get what we expect.

A lot of top performing athletes, Olympic medal winners, are often asked "their secret". The answer? They focus on what they want to happen. When asked of his continuous success as a top ranked hockey player, NHL all star Wayne Gretzky said: "Besides practice, I constantly see the puck where it needs to be."

> **Empowerment Tip**
>
> What are you expecting in regards to the workplace bullying? Even if you feel hopeless and have very little belief that things can be different, try this:
>
> 1. Act on the above steps anyway
>   - Be aware of what you do not want
>   - Replace what you don't want with what you do want.
>   - Create the belief – see it.
>
> 2. Resist the mental and emotional gymnastics of rationalization.

CHAPTER 10

Bully Free At Work™: What Employers Can Do About Workplace Bullying

> **Overview**
>
> 1. What Makes an Organization Vulnerable to Bullying?
> 2. Workplace Bullying: The Aftermath
> 3. What Employers Can Do
> 4. Generating a Bully Free At Work ™ Policy in Your Workplace

1. What Makes an Organization Vulnerable to Bullying?

There is no single profile of an organization that is more vulnerable to bullying than another. The truth is workplace bullying can occur anywhere. But there are certain factors that foster bullying. According to Davenport et al, poor management (including weak leadership, highly hierarchical structures, an excessive bottom-line orientation and no open door policy), a high stress or monotonous environment, and unethical activities provide fertile breeding grounds for bullying to operate, unchecked. [19]

The toll of bullying on an individual can be enormous. And it is also a huge liability for employers. An obvious cost is

---

19   Davenport et al, 1999. pp. 66-69.

productivity, as the performance of employees being bullied will almost certainly suffer. Once an important asset of the organization, the employee being bullied is now a liability, an accident waiting to happen, a lawsuit waiting to be filed. And the effects of bullying don't stop with just that employee. The workplace, once agreeable, cooperative and productive, becomes increasingly tense and suspicious. Small conflicts erupt here and there. As work quality and teamwork goes down, absenteeism, accident rates, conflicts and turnover go up. Employees once loyal to the company become resentful. The best employees begin to leave, and the organization is left with only the mediocre. Oh, and the bullies.

2. Workplace Bullying: The Aftermath

If you drive a nail into a wall and pull the nail out, there is still a hole left in the wall. If you wish to fill the hole with putty, you can have a brand new wall.

With workplace bullying, it is not so simple; filling the hole with putty is more of a "bandage" as opposed to a healing.

Whether you've been a target, or work or have worked with someone who has been a target of workplace bullying, take note: even though the nail, i.e., the bullying, may have been taken "out", the hole may very well still be there.

The lead-up to workplace bullying: what happens?

1. An individual is targeted: usually someone who is kind, caring, smart, and often has a solid work performance.

2. The bully begins to separate the target from others in order to purposefully attack the target.

3. Tactics such as exclusion, unreasonable demands, unfairness, verbal abuse and "crazy-making" are used to disempower the target.

4. Other employees are affected, but do not say anything; they are not sure what to do or say. They end up by not offering support, and the bullying behavior is tolerated.

5. The organization and the bully minimize the impact the target feels, and may even start to blame the target for poor performance.

6. The behavior becomes part of the cultural norm: "This is the way it is around here."

7. Leadership and Human Resources do not know what to do. They ignore the problem. This allows the behavior to continue.

8. The organizational culture starts to break down. Employees become distant, silent and non-creative.

9. The target suffers emotionally, physically and spiritually. The target eventually quits (80% of the time).

10. Nothing is said publicly after the target leaves.

Most organizations do not have pro-active education and accountability plans in place to prevent workplace bullying, or to support the target and ultimately the culture.

After the target leaves: what happens at work?

1. Co-workers of the target try to forget what happened. They feel helpless; ignoring the problem seems like the only way to deal with it.

2. The bully finds a new target.

3. The bully is sometimes even promoted for getting rid of the "problem" person who was not performing.

After the target leaves: what happens for the target?

1. The target is suffering physically, emotionally, and spiritually; in many cases, he is not able to move onto a new job.

2. The target's family and friends are relieved that the target has left the workplace, thinking. "This will be the end of it."

3. The target's family and friends want to move on; they may withdraw their support for the target out of exhaustion. They are also not sure what to do.

4. The target feels "I should be over it," since he has finally left the situation, and it took so long to make the decision to leave. He wants an immediate result of relief.

5. The target does not get needed support for the "aftermath" of being bullied.

6. The target may experience long term suffering, such as irregular sleep, stress disorders and depression.

Did you know...that Heinz Leyman, a Swedish doctor and researcher, worked with victims of workplace mobbing doing healing and research? He found the targets' chances of healing were reduced if the perpetrator went unpunished and the target was not properly supported. If the target felt that his safety was still in question, the chances of healing were reduced.

Here is what to do after a target leaves:

1. Know that if you have been a target of workplace bullying, you have every right to take the time to grieve and heal properly.

2. Seek professional help with a counselor who is experienced in dealing with emotional trauma.

3. As a target's friend, co-worker or family member, seek to support the target by encouraging his healing, through listening and being empathetic to his needs. You may even want to go for coaching yourself in order to know "how to best support".

4. If someone has left work due to being bullied, know that nothing will change unless co-workers band together to create change. At the very least, ask for Workplace Bullying Awareness Training in order to know what your rights and options are, and what to do if you face this behavior again. Knowledge is power.

5. If someone has left your workplace due to being a target of workplace bullying, remember it has been a long difficult battle for him in many ways. He will feel rejected, unsupported, alone and very stressed. At the very least, offer your empathetic support to him verbally or in written form...this is a life line that will go a long way!

3. What Employers Can Do

Bullies cannot flourish – in fact, they cannot even survive – in organizations committed to respect, open communication, and teamwork among employees. A would-be target has an abundance of support in this type of environment, while the bully has none.

Here are the minimum steps an employer should be taking:

Clarify and communicate organization's values.

Clarify what your organization's values are in regard to treating employees with dignity and respect. Reaffirm your organization's commitment to this regularly: in company newsletters, employee handbooks, memos, in meetings, etc. It is most helpful if employees are involved with creating these values or re-committing or renewing their values to each other periodically. This creates a better buy-in. Ask "What do these behaviors - such as respect, positive attitude, support and team work - look like?" This way employees become aware of the specific behaviors that are acceptable or not acceptable.

Use managers as role models.

Recognize that your supervisors and managers are role models. Make sure they are modelling values consistent with your organization's values. If they do not exemplify high standards in respect, honesty, open communication and other interpersonal skills, they need to be held accountable to these values. The first step is: Are the managers and supervisors actually aware and trained in this area? Second step: If they are aware and are still not proficient interpersonally, then coaching can assist with the behavioral change. The coaching can be done by one's boss if the boss is trained in coaching skills, or by an outside interpersonal effectiveness coach. If the person is still not able to be an effective role model, then perhaps he or she is not the best match for the organization. Weigh interpersonal effectiveness heavily when evaluating their performance.

Develop open communication between management and employees.

Engender trust between management and employees. Tell (and keep reminding) employees that they may come to management and Human Resources to speak confidentially about bullying and other issues of concern. Encourage them to speak up about being bullied, even if they're not sure if that's what is happening.

This can be a bit tricky because, if a manager or Human Resources person becomes aware of harassment or potential harm to an employee, they have the responsibility to take corrective action. They can handle this by outlining the limits of confidentiality in a discussion with an employee before it begins, as counselors do. For example, "Thank you for coming to talk with me. I assure you I will keep what we speak about completely confidential. Let me say up front though, that there is one circumstance where I cannot keep it confidential. That is, if harassment is going on or there is the potential harm to an employee. Then I would need to take action and would have to share what you're saying."

Provide a complaint process.

Have a structured complaint process, and make sure employees are aware of it and how it works. They should understand it in detail to allay concerns about confidentiality, documentation in their files, etc. If yours is a large organization, you might designate employees whose role is to investigate instances of possible bullying.

Train managers and employees about bullying.

Provide training to your managers, supervisors and employees about bullying and harassment. Make sure they understand that the organization is committed to a work environment that respects the dignity of all employees. Employees should be trained about their role as a bystander if they witness bullying behavior.

Support interpersonal skills training for employees.

Encourage employees to attend interpersonal skills training, especially in the areas of assertiveness skills, self-esteem building, decision-making skills and effective communication. Do this by paying for or subsidizing the cost of the training. "The only thing worse than training your employees and having them leave is not training them and having them stay!" (Zig Ziglar).

Punish bullies.

Take action with the bully, levying the appropriate penalty, such as suspension, reassignment or termination. If the behavior doesn't warrant termination, you need to make sure it's corrected. Enroll him in counselling and/or serious remedial training that includes interpersonal, assertiveness, anger management and communication skills. Monitor his behavior.

Don't hire bullies.

That might sound pretty obvious, but I mean make a concerted effort during the recruitment process to spot candidates who exhibit aggression. Asking people about their values in the interview process is helpful. Also asking them to share their thoughts on bullying and bullying behavior might give you further insights.

Conduct an employee survey.

Consider conducting an employee survey to uncover, among other valuable information, instances and patterns of bullying. Such a survey must have strong confidentiality mechanisms (probably administered by an outside firm). Find out how employees rate their departments for such things as being treated with respect, feeling valued, honest and open communication, and so forth.

4. Generating a "Bully Free At Work ™" Policy in Your Workplace

Adopt an anti-bullying policy if you don't already have one. An anti-harassment policy isn't enough: make sure it covers bullying, using the specific word bullying.

Too much freedom is bondage! Freedom from having any policies with regard to stopping bullying in the workplace and "hoping for the best", i.e., that people will conduct themselves in an inter-personal way that is appropriate and respectful, is leaving a lot to chance. We must protect even the best of workplace cultures; remember 1 out of 6 people are bullied at work.

Here is a step by step system you can use to instigate a "Bully Free At Work ™" Policy where you work:

1. Gather a group (or groups) of employees and ask them "What type of behavior would you like to see at

work?" For example: respectful, dignity based, inclusive, supportive, honoring. Make the list as long as possible.

2. If you are having trouble making this list, then start with the behaviors you do not want to see at work such as: disrespectful, condescending, argumentative...and then ask: "What would we like instead?" This will help you to decide the behaviors you do want.

3. Remember: Stating what you want is key; then it is easier to create a standard. Make sure this step is done well.

4. Make a list of the behaviors you do not want: the bullying behaviors.

5. Go back to your list of the behaviors you do want and outline what each of these looks like. For example: Inclusiveness means to ask others to participate, not leaving them out when they should be involved in decisions for work.

6. Come up with a clear statement that your workplace will not tolerate bullying. Define bullying as: repeated, disrespectful behavior toward another with an intention of harm.

7. What are the consequences if someone is caught bullying? For example: Bullying is a dismissal offence. This states what you will do if someone is found guilty of bullying.

8. Nominate a senior person in the workplace who will be the "go-to" person when bullying occurs; and empower everyone to speak up if they witness such (agreed upon) behavior.

9. Indicate an open policy where all workers are able to approach this person, should they find themselves being

bullied; and assure that all claims will be looked into. Coach people to come informed and having documented the behavior they have witnessed: how they felt, what it caused them to do as a result, and how it has harmed the workplace.

10. Promote and reward positive workplace behaviors and review your policy and procedures often by asking your employees how they can be improved.

Having clear guidelines provides leadership with regard to stopping workplace bullying.

Worried about the next steps? Make a copy of this page and share it with your manager or a manager at work and suggest you have someone come in to facilitate this discussion. You deserve to be part of a healthy workplace culture.

What must happen in order to ensure workplace bullying policies are not only created but followed through?

1. The organization must become aware of workplace bullying through education.

2. The organization must decide and agree upon what type of culture they want.

3. The organization must decide and agree on what workplace behaviors they do not want.

4. The organization must agree to hold workplace bullies accountable for their behavior.

Workplace bullying policy creation and enforcement is everyone's responsibility.

Who must be held accountable in order to ensure workplace bullying policies are respected?

1. Employees: Accountable to the organization to learn and retain workplace bullying education in order to be empowered to protect a bully-free workplace. Accountable to the target, should the target need support; by listening to what the target has to say, and not ignoring or further excluding the target.

2. Managers/Boss: Accountable to supporting the target by hearing and listening to the target, acknowledging the target's feelings and personal perception of the experience (empathy) and moving toward resolution by getting the clear statement of facts from the target.

3. Targets: Accountable to themselves by naming the problem instead of ignoring it, stating the problem by documentation, creating a support system and keeping their health levels up in order to be resilient to move through to a solution.

With confrontational situations such as bullying in the workplace, the temptation is to ignore the problem. This is denial, and denial will only perpetuate the situation. Leadership and empowerment are key to solving workplace bullying situations.

What can employees, co-workers and peers do when witnessing bullying behavior toward a target?

1. Approach the target and offer your empathetic support and understanding.

2. Encourage the target to start naming the behavior as workplace bullying.

3. Encourage the target to start stating the behavior in order to document and prove the situation.

4. Encourage and even accompany the target to talk to a manager or boss (one's direct report).

5. Continue to check in with the target for support.

Co-worker support is key to a target's effectiveness in facing workplace bullying behavior. This is no time to ignore the problem.

What can a manager or boss do to help stop workplace bullying?

1. Be on the lookout for employees that may be targets and have not been confident enough to say anything; or aware enough to address the situation. Sometimes the bully is the target's boss: peer managers must be able to help coach in these situations.

2. Ask the target "Is there anything I can do to help you ensure your work experience is going well?"

3. Create a safe environment, sharing with the target "There are no wrong or bad answers."

4. Ask the target "Is there anything you wish were different at work?"

5. Write down the target's feedback as a sign of respect that you are willing to listen (creates safety).

6. Paraphrase/repeat back what you have heard the target say, in order for the target to feel understood by you.

7. Work toward receiving documentation (the statement) from the target.

8. You may choose to encourage the target to speak to the bully (in minor and moderate bullying situations).

9. For severe bullying, the boss needs to step in to address the bullying behavior, using the "Classy crucial conversations that count" planner with the bully (and target present) for a three-way intervention; with the goal of gaining an agreement from the bully.

10. Continue to check in with the target to see if the agreement has been kept; continue to encourage the target's growth and protection from the workplace bully.

A manager's role and support is perhaps the most important role for any target of workplace bullying, because managers actually have the power to enforce action and accountability.

Why commit to stopping workplace bullying?

Employers and managers should know that eighty percent of targets who do not receive support end up by leaving the organization. These are often dedicated, loyal and hardworking employees. Once these people start to leave, other employees may follow. It's that simple: stopping this behavior requires management intervention and leadership. For targets, know you have every right to be treated with respect. Keep studying, reading and working through the process of claiming your power back – you will make it.
For the community at large – workplace bullying can be prevented and stopped. It is everyone's responsibility. It takes courage, commitment and accountability. It will take all of us for each of us to make the difference.

Conclusion

Well, we have certainly covered a lot, haven't we? And if you have done the exercises and assignments in each chapter, you have already accomplished a great deal, by focusing on the person who matters most – not the bully, but *you*. Getting to know yourself, becoming skilled at taking care of yourself, learning to ask for what you need – and figuring out what that is in the first place!

I hope you feel good about the groundwork you have laid for yourself so far. You have greater understanding about what bullying is. You've learned to identify whether or not you are being bullied and, hopefully have gained insight into ways to insulate yourself from being harassed. You have a much clearer understanding about how being bullied can harm you emotionally, mentally and physically, as well as how to protect yourself from bullying and minimize its effects even if you can't always completely stop the behavior. You are now familiar with the four-step response to bullying: stating the problem, protecting yourself, empowering yourself, and taking action.

We delved deeply into the concept of wellness, that wonderful state of health and contentment in body, mind and spirit. Assignments and exercises in this book equipped you with tools to empower yourself, manage your stress level, engage support, communicate openly and effectively about your needs, and make good decisions. Hopefully, as you have taken a fresh new look at your unique gifts, talents, skills and personal traits, you have experienced a new-found appreciation and sense of worth for yourself. You have assessed your assertiveness level and have developed a structured plan to respond in a healthily assertive manner to bullying – and to life's challenges, in general. Finally, we examined the practical aspects of your situation to help you evaluate your alternatives, decide what steps to take, and to improve your options.

You might feel like you're ready to confront the bully. And maybe you are. But, as I said, I think that what you've done is to lay the groundwork, the all-important foundation from which you will derive your strength and resiliency.

Meanwhile, please continue with the exercises and assignments in this book. Be diligent! It takes a lot of repetition to replace the old "programming" we've been running on all our lives with new, better approaches. So, practice the principles we've discussed here and continue to build your self-esteem and develop your assertiveness. Continue increasing your overall state of wellness, becoming stronger and more resilient all the time. If you are just out of – or still going through – a bullying experience, give your mind, heart and body a little time to recharge.

Once your energy is up again, you will be ready to learn specific strategies and tactics for triumphing over a bully. *How to Have a Bully Free Workplace* will be published soon. You'll learn when and how to enlist your manager's help and what to do if your manager doesn't know how to handle the bully. You'll find out in more detail what your options are, and how to expand them even further.

How to Have a Bully Free Workplace will also be a practical guide for managers, supervisors, employees and Human Resources people who want to ensure a work environment that honours and dignifies all employees and that does not tolerate bullying. The book will include a comprehensive audit checklist to determine if your workplace is vulnerable to bullying, or possibly already under siege. It will cover in depth what actions to take to create a Bully Free At Work™ environment and to dismantle the structures and circumstances that enable a bully to operate. It will provide specific guidance and resources about how to create a healthful, productive work environment that is a pleasure for employees to operate in.

So, watch for this new book in the months ahead. Meanwhile, I hope this one continues to give you the inspiration, guidance and support you seek so that you can live a life you enjoy.

Appendix

Self-Tests, Assignments and Exercises

Overview

1. Self-Test: Are You Being Bullied?
2. Self-Test: Are You Wearing a Bull's Eye on Your Back?
3. Self-Test: How Bullying Is Affecting You
4. Assignment: Stating the Problem
5. Exercise: Casting Yourself Forward One Year
6. Exercise: Wellness Wheel
7. Assignment: Action Plan to Improve Physical Health
8. Assignment: Identifying Calming Activities
9. Exercise: Reframing Negative Thoughts
10. Assignment: Action Plan to Reduce Stress
11. Assignment: Identifying Your Support Team
12. Exercise: Rosenberg Self-Esteem Scale
13. Assignment: Identify Your Strengths
14. Assignment: Decision-Making Step #1—Identify Your Options
15. Self-Test: How Assertive Are You?
16. Assignment: Responding Assertively
17. Assignment: Daily Debriefing
18. Assignment: Preparing to Leave
19. Assignment: Decision-Making Step #2—Evaluating Your Options
20. Assignment: Decision-Making Step #3—Choose an Option

1. Self-Test: Are You Being Bullied?

Consider each of the questions in the self-test below and decide if you Strongly Agree, Somewhat Agree, Disagree, or Strongly Disagree. Then, circle the corresponding number.

Does the person you're having challenges with:	Strongly Agree	Agree	Somewhat Agree	Disagree	Strongly Disagree
1. Ignore you. Not say hello when you greet them. Not return phone calls or emails.	5	4	3	2	1
2. Dismiss what you're saying or "put you down" while alone or in the presence of others?	5	4	3	2	1
3. Sabotage you or make you look foolish, such as "forgetting" to tell you about meetings (or) if the person is your boss, set you up to fail by making impossible demands of you?	6	5	4	3	2
4. Spread rumours, lies and half-truths about you?	6	5	4	3	2
5. Frequently act impatient with you, treating you like you're incompetent?	5	4	3	2	1
6. Routinely blame and criticize you?	5	4	3	2	1

Does the person you're having challenges with:		Strongly Agree	Agree	Somewhat Disagree	Disagree	Strongly Disagree
7.	Try to intimidate you by interrupting, contradicting, glaring, acting forceful or giving you the silent treatment?	5	4	3	2	1
8.	Ridicule, insult or play tricks on you, especially in front of others?	6	5	4	3	2
9.	Always insist on getting their own way and never apologizing?	5	4	3	2	1
10.	Leave you out of social and work situations as opposed to inviting or including you?	6	5	4	3	2
	Total score = _____ (Possible total of 54)	Now add your score.				

Remember, workplace bullying can be tough to measure because of its subjectivity. Bullying occurs when a target experiences repeated disrespectful behavior. These are (some) of the top disrespectful behaviors experienced by targets and know there are more. This self-test is primarily designed to help you name and become more aware of any severity.

If your score is 24 or below, it doesn't look like you're being bullied. If your score is between 25 and 34, there are indications of bullying behavior. If your score is 35 or above, you are definitely being bullied.

2. Self-Test: Are You Wearing a Bull's Eye on Your Back?

How vulnerable to a bully attack are you? Rate yourself on the following characteristics below to find out. Be as honest and objective as you can be.

Personality characteristics
(circle one number for each characteristic)

Timid: Do you tend to be timid; hate confrontations; strongly prefer safe, routine situations? Or are you more assertive, asking for what you want, sticking up for yourself when necessary, but still disliking confrontation? Or are you downright bold, aggressive at times, don't mind confrontations?

Timid		Assertive		Aggressive
5	4	3	2	1

Do you bend over backwards to accommodate others, even to a point of being a sucker sometimes? Are you cooperative, as long as you're sure the other party also wants a win-win? Or are you competitive, needing to win at any cost?

Rescuing		Cooperative		Competitive
5	4	3	2	1

Are you totally "up front," 100% truthful no matter what, and tend to expect others to be the same, often confused when they're not? Are you generally honest and direct, but take some care about the effects of what you're saying? Or are you shrewd, good at figuring out how to manoeuvre the best outcome for yourself?

Honest to a fault		Direct and open		Shrewd
5	4	3	2	1

Do you get really worked up when someone is treated unfairly, even if you don't particularly care for the person? Or are you more generally fair-minded, but still don't mind when people you like (or yourself) get an extra advantage? Or do you consider a good outcome to be one where you get what you want?

Crusader of justice		Fair-minded		Self-serving
5	4	3	2	1

Are you a sucker, believing everything you're told by everyone? Do you, while maintaining an open mind, consider the motives of the person telling you something, as well as their knowledge of the matter? Or is your first reaction to almost everything suspicion, believing that people mainly say and do things for their own gain?

Gullible		Open-minded		Cynical
5	4	3	2	1

Do you instantly "feel" the hurt when you see someone in pain, and be able to automatically put yourself in their shoes, sometimes feeling that you are carrying the burdens of the world? Do you try to be considerate of others' needs and feelings, but not to a point where it interferes with your life? Do you pride yourself for telling it like it is, although people who are "too sensitive" often take offence?

Empathetic		Considerate		Insensitive
5	4	3	2	1

Do you tend to do anything to accommodate others, even if very inconvenient for you and you suspect it won't be appreciated? Are you happy to oblige someone, as long as it isn't a big inconvenience? Do you make sure you take care of "Number One," and not worry about whether others are satisfied?

Over-obliging		Cooperative		Self-centered
5	4	3	2	1

3. Self-Test: How Bullying Is Affecting You

Do you know how bullying is affecting you? Look at the following table, which is an abbreviated list of the adverse effects of bullying, and place a checkmark next to the effects that you're experiencing.

How Bullying Is Affecting Me	Me (normally)	Me (being bullied)
Physical symptoms:		
Headaches	☐	☐
Sore muscles	☐	☐
Jitteriness	☐	☐
Nervousness	☐	☐
Gritting teeth (sore jaw)	☐	☐
Heartburn	☐	☐
Indigestion	☐	☐
Decreased/increased appetite	☐	☐
Light-headedness	☐	☐
Racing pulse	☐	☐
Increased blood pressure	☐	☐
Chest pain	☐	☐
Heart palpitations	☐	☐
Unable to get to sleep	☐	☐
Unable to stay asleep	☐	☐
Fatigue/exhaustion	☐	☐
Decreased sex drive	☐	☐
Weight gain/loss	☐	☐
Skin breakouts	☐	☐
Hair loss	☐	☐
Increased sweating	☐	☐
Nausea	☐	☐

How Bullying Is Affecting Me	Me (normally)	Me (being bullied)
Emotional symptoms:		
Depression	☐	☐
Anxiety	☐	☐
Feelings of dread	☐	☐
Fear	☐	☐
Panic attacks	☐	☐
Sadness	☐	☐
Moodiness	☐	☐
Anger	☐	☐
Numbness	☐	☐
Feelings of hopelessness	☐	☐
Guilt	☐	☐
Dread going to work	☐	☐
Don't care about anything	☐	☐
Feelings of shame	☐	☐
Feelings of worthlessness	☐	☐
Thoughts of suicide	☐	☐
Paranoia	☐	☐
Jitteriness	☐	☐
Tearfulness	☐	☐
Feeling like screaming	☐	☐
Mental symptoms:		
Confusion	☐	☐
Forgetfulness	☐	☐
Disorientation	☐	☐
Inability to concentrate	☐	☐
Difficulty making simple decisions	☐	☐

How Bullying Is Affecting Me	Me (normally)	Me (being bullied)
Nightmares	☐	☐
Obsession over bullying situation	☐	☐
Brain lockup (Unable to think)	☐	☐
Flashbacks	☐	☐
Negative thoughts	☐	☐
Behavioral symptoms:		
Isolating myself from others	☐	☐
Becoming dependent on others	☐	☐
Becoming withdrawn from friends and loved ones	☐	☐
Fighting with loved ones	☐	☐
Neglecting my appearance	☐	☐
Neglecting my health (diet, exercise, sleep)	☐	☐
Increased alcohol/drug use	☐	☐
Poor work performance	☐	☐
Neglect of financial matters	☐	☐
Neglect of pets	☐	☐
Increased smoking	☐	☐
Risky behavior	☐	☐
Obsessive behaviors	☐	☐
Increasing inability to go to or remain at work	☐	☐
Reliance on sleep aids and tranquilizers	☐	☐
Unable to motivate myself	☐	☐

4. Assignment: Stating the Problem

If you recall from Chapter 1, the definition of bullying has two main parts, the action (repeated, deliberate, disrespectful behavior) and the effect (harm to the target). At this point, you have a pretty good idea about whether or not you are being bullied (see Self-test, Are you being bullied? in Chapter 2) and you understand how it is harming you (see Self-test, How bullying is affecting me, in Chapter 4). Now it's time to put your statement of the problem in writing.

You'll need a blank journal or notebook for the following assignment and for other entries and assignments as you work through the processes in this book.

> On a blank page in your journal, write "Statement of Problem" at the top. Then describe the parts of the problem:
> - **Who** is doing the bullying?
> - **What** does the behavior consist of?
> - **How often** does the bullying occur? Can you show that it is repeated?
> - **What are the effects** of the bullying on you? Your statement should be short, possibly one to three sentences. It is not necessary to add details.

Stating the problem is the first step in deciding how to handle it. Later in this book, you will identify your options, evaluate them and, finally, decide what you want to do. For now, though, I'll just ask you to create headings for the other decision-making steps, and leave the pages blank.

Below your statement of the problem, write the following headings for the next three pages:

"Options" - Leave the rest of the page blank for now.
"Evaluate Options", next line: "Pros:" and "Cons".
"Choose an Option" - Identify actions to address obstacles.

Example: Statement of problem

Who: Paul Harwood

What/How Often: Makes fun of me in front of others by pre-calling poor job performance on my part; not giving me specific deadlines and then saying I was late turning in my project. Each time I've been in contact this past week, an incident such as above has occurred.

The Effects: This is causing me insomnia; and it is hard to concentrate on my job. I also feel left out and demoralized, and am beginning to doubt my own abilities.

Step #1:   Options (leave rest of page blank)

Step #2:   Evaluate Options
             Pros: Cons:
             (leave rest of page blank)

Step #3:   Choose Option - Identify action steps to
             address any obstacles.

             (leave rest of page blank)

5. Exercise: Casting Yourself Forward One Year

Imagine yourself sitting with a friend, maybe over lunch, one year from now. Invent your conversation, something along this line:

Friend: "You've had quite a year."
You: "I sure have. I never thought I'd survive all that business with (name of the person who is bullying you)."
Friend: "How did that all work out, anyway?"
You: (Describe one possible version of how it was resolved, such as that you eventually confronted the bully and he finally backed down, that Human Resources facilitated a conflict resolution process between you two, that you decided to leave the company, etc.)
Friend: "Oh, so you did do that after all. The last time we talked, you didn't want to take that step."
You: "Yeah, but I realized it was the best thing to do…and it turned out really well."
Friend: "Wow, it must have been scary for you."
You: "Yes, I was scared to death (to stand up to the bully, that you wouldn't be able to get a new job, that your partner wouldn't be supportive, etc.). But it wasn't that hard after all. It's never as bad as you think it might be."
Friend: "And look at you now—you seem so happy….in fact, centered and less stressed - attractive!"
You: "I am. Things worked out a lot better than I thought they would. That doesn't mean things are perfect. (You describe that you and the bully still avoid each other, or that you have a longer commute on your new job, etc.). But it's much better than it was. I don't blame myself; I almost can't believe I did it! Everything is going much better."
Friend: "You know, I admire you very much."
You: "Thanks. I feel pretty proud of myself, too."

6. Exercise: Wellness Wheel

You can do this exercise by printing out the pages of the abbreviated Wellness Wheel, available at no charge at www.wright.edu/admin/wellness/wellnesswheel.htm.
Or you can look at the wellness wheel in Chapter 6 and draw it in your journal. Mark the various aspects of the wheel as indicated and then color in at what level you would rate yourself. Coloring right to the outer edge of the circle would indicate satisfaction, with where you are at in this area.

With either version of the Wellness Wheel, score yourself and plot your scores on the wheel.

Look at your wheel. How balanced is it? Any surprises? Now ask yourself what would be your top three areas for improvement. What activities or steps could you take to round out your wheel? Having a full and balanced wheel is really saying that you have a high level of resilience - exactly what you need for self preservation against the effects of bullying.

7. Assignment: Action Plan to Improve Physical Health

Write "Action plan to improve eating, breathing, moving and sleeping habits" on a blank page in your journal. Write down at least three ways you intend to improve your health habits.

Example: Action plan to improve eating, breathing, moving and sleeping habits
Bring healthy bag lunch 2 times per week.
Eat at least 6 servings of vegetables and fruit every day!
Have no more than one soda per day.
Take 5 minutes out each day for deep breathing.
Climb stairs to office rather than taking elevator.
15 minute stretches every weekday morning. Go to bed by 10pm Sun-Thurs.

8. Assignment: Identifying Calming Activities

Write "Activities that bring me peace of mind" on a blank page in your journal. Think about the activities that calm your soul, and write them down. List as many as you can. Try to list at least three or four that you can easily do every day.

Example:
Activities That Bring Me Peace of Mind:
1. Hiking
2. Taking my dog for a walk
3. Cup of tea
4. Warm bath
5. Jazz
6. Massage
7. Meditating/prayer
8. Affirmation tapes
9. Poetry – reading, writing
10. Inspiring movies
11. Talking with Mom
12. Running, working out
13. Being still
14. Gardening
15. Cooking

9. Exercise: Reframing Negative Thoughts

Make two columns on a blank page of your journal and write the headings, "Negative Thought" and "Reframed Thought." Write down a negative thought, either just as you become aware of it or later, when you think back on your day. Then, reframe the thought in your mind. What is the real truth about this issue that I'm worried or upset about? The reframed thoughts in my example below are brief, but feel free to expand on the reframed thought as much as you want – you might even want to write an action plan!

Example:

Negative Thought:	Reframed Thought:
I just can't handle this!	This is difficult but I can handle it.
No one cares about me.	Lots of people care about me, especially Jon, Sheila and Sandy.
Oh my god, I'll never be able to pay my bills this month.	I'm scared about my money situation. Let me sit down and work out how I can manage it. Others have; I can, too.

10. Assignment: Action Plan to Reduce Stress

Review your Wellness Wheel scores and the exercises you've completed and notes you have written about nurturing yourself (identifying the activities that calm your mind), meditating, regulating your breathing, not multitasking, and reframing negative thinking.

Now you're ready to formulate an action plan. Write "Action plan to reduce stress" on a blank page in your journal. You might need to devote two or more pages to this assignment. Write down actions that you will commit to doing in order to reduce your stress level. Ideally, your list will contain something from each of the areas above.

Example:
Action Plan to Reduce Stress

Hiking – Do one evening hike and one day hike a week
Meditate 20 minutes every day, first thing in the morning.
Work out at gym 3 times a week.
Garden 2 hours on the weekend.
Listen to music instead of watching TV one night per week.
Get a massage this week.
Cook a dinner from scratch for yourself or a friend once this week.
Go to bed by 10pm.
Rent a comedy DVD once a week and actually watch it!
Make to-do list each day for next day. Focus on one task at a time.

11. Assignment: Identifying Your Support Team

Write "My potential support team" on a blank page in your journal. Then sit and brainstorm everyone who might be able to offer some kind of help to you, however minor. You might envision having a heart-to-heart conversation with one member of your support team, and ask for advice on a specfic issue from another.

Another element in having a strong support team is how well you open yourself up to the support that is being offered. For instance, are you comfortable seeking help when you need it, or would you rather "go it alone?" Do you appreciate honest feedback, or does it often make you feel criticized?

12. Exercise: Rosenberg Self-Esteem Scale

Below is a list of statements dealing with your general feelings about yourself. Consider each statement and, without thinking too long about your response, decide if you strongly agree, agree, disagree or strongly disagree. Then circle the corresponding number. When you're finished, total up the numbers. Your total should be between 0 and 30.

Rosenberg Self-Esteem Scale		Strongly Agree	Agree	Disagree	Strongly Disagree
1.	I feel that I'm a person of worth, at least on an equal plane with others.	3	2	1	0
2.	I feel that I have a number of good qualities.	3	2	1	0
3.	All in all, I am inclined to feel that I am a failure.	0	1	2	3
4.	I am able to do things as well as most other people.	3	2	1	0
5.	I feel I do not have much to be proud of.	0	1	2	3
6.	I take a positive attitude toward myself.	3	2	1	0
7.	On the whole, I am satisfied with myself.	3	2	1	0
8.	I wish I could have more respect for myself.	0	1	2	3
9.	I certainly feel useless at times.	0	1	2	3
10.	At times I think I am no good at all.	0	1	2	3
	Total score = _____				

Interpreting the Rosenberg Self-Esteem Scale

Dr. Rosenberg did not use specific cut-off points to designate low, average and high self-esteem. I feel that a score of 18 or below indicates low self-esteem, 19 to 25 indicates average self-esteem, and 26 and above indicates high self-esteem.

13. Assignment: Identify Your Strengths

The first step in focusing on and building your strengths is, of course, to identify them.

At the top of a blank page of your journal, write "My Strengths", then make three headings, "Personality and Character Traits," "Physical Characteristics," and "Talents and Aptitudes," leaving enough space after each heading to fill in details. (See example below.)

Next, make up a similar form on a blank of sheet of paper and make several photocopies. Give these copies to people who know you well, and ask them to complete it. Let them know you're working on a project for your self-reflection. Ask them to take the worksheet with them and complete it when they can devote a little time to thinking about it. Emphasize that it is their honest opinions that will be of most help to you.

Consider the headings on the "My Strengths" page in your journal, and taking a few days to reflect, write down what you think your strengths are. Write down even those qualities that you think are "no big deal." Remember, all of us and especially people with low self-esteem tend to discount our good points.

When you've gotten the worksheets back, compare those observations with your own. Are there some differences? Do others notice and appreciate strengths in you that you yourself don't see?

Add your family's and friend's observations to your own list.

Set aside some time and really consider the qualities that others and you recognize in you. Do this often. And always feel free to add more strengths as they occur to you!

Example:

My Strengths:

Personality and character traits:	
• Honest • Caring • Responsible • Smart • Hard-working • Loyal • Patient • Fun-loving	• Good listener • Dependable • Good sense of humour • Open-minded • Flexible • Disciplined (determined) • Tidy • Methodical
Physical Traits:	
• Nice smile/nice face • Good health/rarely sick • Takes care of self	• Strong/has endurance • Good eye contact • Lots of energy
Talents and Aptitudes:	
• Good cook • Likes to entertain • Handy around the house • Plays guitar well • Sings pretty well	• Wide range of interests • Good outdoors person • Athletic – run, ski, bike • Great storyteller • Good with kids & animals
Personal Gifts to Share, Develop and Acquire:	
• Caring/patient/great storyteller – volunteer at a senior's center? • Fun-loving/good cook/entertain – have friends over more? • Good listener – get closer with Dave. • Handy around the house – make to-do list and get busy! • Good with kids – have niece and nephew over more often. • Good with animals – volunteer at an animal shelter?	

14. Assignment: Decision-Making Step #1—Identify Your Options

Go to the "Statement of Problem/Options" page in your journal. Write down every option (and variation) you can think of. Don't evaluate them yet; just keeping writing whatever comes into your mind. Talk with your support team and get their ideas, too. I will ask you to come back and complete Steps #2 and #3 a little later.

Example:
Statement of Problem:

Who: Paul Harwood

What/How Often: Makes fun of me in front of others by pre-calling poor job performance on my part; not giving me specific deadlines and then saying I was late turning in my project. Each time I've been in contact this past week, an incident such as above has occurred.

The Effects: This is causing me insomnia; and it is hard to concentrate on my job. I also feel left out and demoralized, and am beginning to doubt my own abilities.

Step #1: Identify Your Options
1. Ignore him.
2. Avoid him.
3. Try harder to get along with him.
4. Talk to him – what is the problem?.
5. Talk to him – ask him to lay off.
6. Threaten to report him.
7. Talk to supervisor.
8. Talk to HR – get advice.
9. Talk to HR – report him.
10. Write note to Paul – ask him to lay off.
11. Ask for transfer out of Warehouse.
12. Campaign – assert myself at every encounter.
13. Look for another job.
14. Take legal action against company.

15. Self-Test: How Assertive Are You?

Consider each of the following statements, then circle the number under the phrase that most closely describes your attitude about it.

How Assertive Are You?		Strongly Agree/ Always	Agree/ Often	Disagree/ Not often	Strongly Disagree/ Never
1.	You feel tense if someone is angry or upset, even if it's not your fault.	0	1	2	3
2.	You can usually say "no" to someone without feeling guilty.	3	2	1	0
3.	You often feel that others take advantage of you.	0	1	2	3
4.	You find it easy to take responsibility for a problem.	3	2	1	0
5.	You often feel hurt that your partner or friend isn't considerate about your needs.	0	1	2	3
6.	You are able to constructively express feelings of anger or frustration to someone close to you, rather than holding the feelings in.	3	2	1	0
7.	You often make excuses to get out of doing something you don't feel like doing.	0	1	2	3

	How Assertive Are You?	Strongly Agree/ Always	Agree/ Often	Disagree/ Not often	Strongly Disagree/ Never
8.	You always stand up for yourself firmly, but respectfully, if someone "crosses the line" with you.	3	2	1	0
9.	You hate confrontations.	0	1	2	3
10.	You see yourself as strong and independent.	3	2	1	0
11.	You feel blamed and criticized by others.	0	1	2	3
12.	You find it easy to make decisions and you trust your own judgment.	3	2	1	0
13.	You feel that people who are assertive are arrogant and superior.	0	1	2	3
14.	When it comes to relationships, you feel there is a good balance of give and take.	3	2	1	0
15.	You envy others who seem more powerful than you.	0	1	2	3

Interpreting the assertiveness self-test

The highest possible score is 45. If your score is between 0 and 18, your tendency is to handle situations very passively (non-assertively). If your score is between 19 and 32, you handle yourself fairly assertively, probably more so in some situations and not so much in others. If your score is between 33 and 45, you don't seem to have any problems asserting yourself.

16. Assignment: Responding Assertively

Think of at least five incidents you have been involved in with another person, in which you responded passively (or aggressively) after which you had hurt or angry feelings. It's better if the incidents don't all involve the same person. It doesn't matter if the exchange happened recently or long ago. Consider interactions with co-workers, your boss, friends, family members, and people you meet incidentally throughout the day, such as store clerks and people you pass on the hiking trail. Also think of the bullying situation you may be in.

For each incident, write a brief description of (1) what the other person did or said that bothered you, and (2) how you responded.

Then, think about and write down how you might have responded more assertively.

Example:

(Other person):	"How many times are you going to ask the same question?" (said in a condescending tone)
Me (actual response):	"Sorry."
Me (assertive response):	"Yes, actually I'm new to this – I'll try and get it as best as I can. I appreciate your help." (Note: this is neither defensive, resentful or pushy. It acknowledges the other person while not backing down).

17. Assignment: Daily Debriefing

Make it a daily practice to review the encounters you had today. Repeat the Responding Assertively exercise you just finished. What did the other person do or say? How did you respond? How might you have responded in a more assertive way, one that respects yourself and the other person? Be easy on yourself – you're just learning this skill!

This will do two amazing things for you in your journey to becoming assertive. First, it will remind you of the basic principles of assertiveness, i.e., respecting yourself and others. Second, it will demonstrate for you that you really do have power, and that asserting this power in a win-win way could bring about different results.

18. Assignment: Preparing to Leave

In this assignment, you will flush out your fears, identify factors that help and hinder you from leaving your work situation, and begin an action plan to correct deficits.

- Find a blank page in your journal and write the heading "Fears." Ask yourself, "What are my very biggest fears at the moment?" and consider this for several minutes. Then jot down a few words to represent your thoughts, such as "losing my job." Probe each fear to uncover a deeper, more basic fear underneath it. For example, losing your job might not bother you if you had another one lined up, so you might write "out of work.....money trouble" and "I'd feel like a failure."

- Next, write the heading "Exit Strategy" and, under that "Assets and Potential Obstacles." What specific skills, knowledge and experience do you have that will help you get your next job? What deficits might you have, such as no resume and not enough money saved? Write down the assets and potential obstacles that come to mind. There is no need for an exhaustive list. It's better to focus on a few important ones.

- Then write "Actions I Will Take." Review each potential obstacle. What you can do about them? Jot down tangible actions that you can take to address each obstacle.

Example:

My Fears
Having to quit job – money trouble – where do I fit in?
Being fired – feel like a failure.
New job – what if I fail – bullies there?

Exit Strategy

Assets	Potential Obstacles
Job:	
7 years experience	No degree
Can work flexible hours	Why I left current job?
Longevity in current job	Outdated resume
Good performance reviews	Not good in interviews
Get along well with others	
Other:	Not enough savings
	Don't know where to start

Actions I Will Take
- No degree – Not huge obstacle. Take courses to update my technical skills.
- How to explain why I left current job – Explore further opportunity, attach a performance review.
- Outdated resume - Ask Sandy to help update.
- Not good at interviews - Get book, ask Sandy to help.
- Not enough savings - Save 3 months more pay. Go on a budget – simplify!
- Don't know where to start - Make list of contacts: friends, people at church, volunteer center - Start looking at job listings - Research companies.

19. Assignment: Decision-Making Step #2—Evaluating Your Options

- Go to the "Step 2 – Evaluate Options" page in your journal.

- Take each option one at a time and consider its pros and cons, based on the information you have at this time. Write them down. Underline the advantages and disadvantages of particular importance to you. If there are obstacles attached to a certain option, make a note. For instance, obstacles associated with the option of looking for a new job might be "outdated resume" and "not enough savings."

- Your options and their pros and cons might seem very obvious to you, so it is vital to talk over your alternatives with your support team. Their objectivity and distance from the situation may steer you to consider an idea that you otherwise might throw out, thinking that "it is no use."

Example:
Statement of Problem:

Who: Paul Harwood

What/How Often: Makes fun of me in front of others by pre-calling poor job performance on my part; not giving me specific deadlines and then saying I was late turning in my project. Each time I've been in contact this past week, an incident such as above has occurred.

The Effects: This is causing me insomnia; and it is hard to concentrate on my job. I also feel left out and demoralized, and am beginning to doubt my own abilities.

Step #1: Identify Your Options
1. Ignore him.
2. Avoid him.
3. Try harder to get along with him.
4. Talk to him – what is the problem?.

5. Talk to him – ask him to lay off.
6. Threaten to report him.
7. Talk to supervisor.
8. Talk to HR – get advice.
9. Talk to HR – report him.
10. Write note to Paul – ask him to lay off.
11. Ask for transfer out of Warehouse.
12. Campaign – assert myself at every encounter.
13. Look for another job.
14. Take legal action against company.

Step #2: Evaluate Your Options	
Pros:	Cons:
1. Ignore	None; things will just get worse.
2. Avoid	Don't have to deal with it – we work too closely.
3. Get along	None; he gets worse when I try.
4. Talk about problem?	Might work it out. Or, he might get worse. He might reject me.
5. Lay off	He might cooperate. Or he might get worse.
6. Threaten	He might stop, might call my bluff or force me to follow through with it. Do I want to?
7. Talk to supervisor.	Might be able to help. He already sees the bullying. I may be seen as a complainer.
8. HR advice	Suggestions? Do something – confidential? I may be seen as a complainer or troublemaker.
9. HR report	Discipline Paul, fire him – things might blow up! Transfer him, transfer me. Paul might wage war.

Pros:	Cons:
10. Write Paul	None; would make things worse.
11. Transfer	No more Paul! Where to? Lose seniority? Stress! New job? Commute, etc. Note: Update resume.
12. Assert myself	Might end problem. Stressful – health? Self-esteem. Note: Need support, training (counselor? training through work?)
13. New job	No more Paul, fresh start. Job? Pay? Commute? How long out of work? Note: Update resume, finish certification.
14. Sue company	None. Things would blow up. Need to report problem first, hard to work there.

20. Assignment: Decision-Making Step #3 —Choose an Option

Once you feel you know all of your options, and have evaluated each of them honestly and objectively, you're ready to decide what action you want to take. Write down your option and include any action items you'll need to address in order to accomplish the option. Remember: Not choosing an option means you will still be in the same place you are at now.

Example:
Step #3: Choose Option (Identify action steps to address any obstacles).

1st choice: Launch campaign to assert myself with Paul. Will need help sticking with this? Look into assertiveness training through company, other assertiveness and self-esteem resources and/or counselling.

2nd choice: Transfer to other department. Do if #1 option doesn't work. Give it 3 months. Meanwhile, update resume and start looking at postings.

Bibliography

1. Adams, Andrea. *Bullying at Work*. London: Virago, 1992.

2. Davenport, Noa Ph.D.; Schwartz, Ruth Distler; Elliott, Gail Pursell. *Mobbing Emotional Abuse in the American Workplace*. Ames, Iowa: Civil Society Publishing. 1999.

3. Field, Tim. *Bully in Sight*. Oxfordshire, UK: Wessex Press, 1996.

4. Goleman, Daniel; Boyatzis, Richard E.; McKee, Annie. *Primal Leadership*. Harvard Business School Press, 2002.

5. Hornstein, Harvey. Ph.D. *Brutal Bosses and Their Prey*. New York: Riverhead Books, 1996.

6. *Wikipedia Online Encyclopedia*, St. Petersburg, FL: Wikipedia Foundation.

7. Workplace Bullying & Trauma Institute, Bellingham, WA. www.bullyinginstitute.org.

8. International Labour Organization. "Violence on the job...a global problem." (Press release.) Geneva, Washington, D.C.: 20 July 1998.

9. Namie, Gary, Ph.D., Namie, Ruth, Ph.D. *The Bully at Work*. Naperville, IL: Sourcebooks, Inc., 2000.

10. Needham, Andrea W. *Workplace Bullying*. Penguin Books, 2003.

11. Randall, Peter. Adult Bullying: *Perpetrators and Victims*. London/New York: Taylor & Francis, 1997.

12. Rayner, Charlotte; Hoel Helge; Cooper, Cary L.; *Workplace Bullying*. London/New York: Taylor & Francis, 2002.

13. Rosenberg, Morris. Society and the Adolescent Self-Image, Rev. Ed. Middletown, CT: Wesleyan University Press, 1989.

14. Selye, Hans, *Stress Without Distress*, New York: New American Library, 1974.

15. *The American Heritage® Stedman's Medical Dictionary*, 2nd Ed., Houghton Mifflin Company, 2004

16. Travis, John W., M.D., *Wellness Inventory*, Asheville, NC: Wellness Associates, 1988.

17. Vaknin, Sam, Ph.D. "Bully at Work: An Interview with Tim Field." The Global Politician, May 28, 2005

About the Author

Valerie Cade has earned world-wide acclaim as a professional speaker and trainer for the past 18 years and is committed to stopping workplace bullying through creating awareness and meeting people "where they are at".

Why? Because she's been there herself. She's experienced firsthand the frustration, shame, and despair of being bullied at work. This fuelled her passion to gather, verify and compile relevant and effective solutions to teach people and companies how to be Bully Free At Work ™.

She has a genuine passion for helping people receive the respect and dignity in the workplace that they deserve.

Valerie's business acumen and speaking experience has come firsthand:

As an Inspirational Speaker and Workplace Bullying Educator:

- Valerie achieved the Certified Speaking Professional Designation (CSP). With less than 900 recipients in the world, this is the highest earned speaking designation worldwide for speaking excellence. She was one of the first females in Canada to earn this designation.

- Valerie is an in-demand speaker throughout the world speaking for all organizations from health care, government, higher education and corporations large and small.

- She is most noted for her engaging approach and personalized delivery that draws audiences into heartfelt action.

As a Leader:

- As a CEO, Valerie strategically turned around two "near bankruptcy" million-dollar companies to very profitable success.
- She is a Past National President for the Canadian Association of Professional Speakers (CAPS); and
- She was presented with the Canadian Association of Professional Speakers (CAPS) President's Award for Distinguished Service, and recently the recipient of the "Spirit of CAPS" award for recognition of her commitment and excellence to the speaking profession. It is the highest peer award in the speaking profession with less than 10 recipients.

As an Expert:

- Valerie was featured on the Healthcare Television Network (U.S. and Europe) for One on One Leadership;

- She is co-author of "Discover Your Inner Strength" with Stephen Covey, Ken Blanchard and Brian Tracy. She is the author of the CD Training Program "Win/Win Assertiveness" and "How to Manage Your Boss." She is also co-author of "Expert Women Who Speak...Speak Out", and of course "Bully Free at Work™", which was noted in Maclean's magazine as an excellent resource to stop workplace bullying.

- As a Professional Speaker and Implementation Specialist, Valerie has worked with people and companies to create lasting change. Most want to change, but actually implementing the change takes a special approach. Her work in creating awareness and implementation with regard to workplace bullying and respectful workplaces has been evidenced in both large and small companies, with outstanding results. Stopping workplace bullying is simply the beginning. Creating a sustainable, respectful workplace where people are inspired to adhere to a higher moral standard is the critical ingredient needed. Creating an inspired system for positive change is Valerie's specialty.

Here is what is available to you should you wish to create workplace bullying awareness, accountability and true change in your organization:

"Bully Free At Work ™: What Is Workplace Bullying and What You Can Do to Stop It?"
This session is excellent for all employees in order to create awareness of workplace bullying. Behaviors, actual workplace situations where bullying is present and what you can do to prevent any disrespectful behavior at work are covered.

"Creating Bully Free At Work™ Policy and Accountability" (for Managers)
For managers and leaders who want to stop disrespectful behavior at work. Creating a system of behavioral awareness and accountability where morale is positive once again.

- Keynote Presentations - To create awareness and hope.
- Seminars - To teach skills.
- Implementation - To create systemic change, awareness, accountability and sustainability.

Contact us anytime at:

Bully Free at Work ™
E-mail: info@bullyfreeatwork.com
Phone: 1.403.508.0678

Also available to you:

Bully Free in a Box™
This is perfect for a department or a group of interested individuals. You receive 20 Bully Free At Work books such as the one you have here PLUS the Bully Free At Work DVD which is 49 minutes of information and inspiration delivered live right to your group! Go to www.BullyFreeAtWork.com to learn more and have your box shipped today.

Bully Free At Work™: The Weekly Tip
Receive our FREE 5 Step Video eCourse on how you can understand and stop workplace bullying. With excellent viewership world-wide it is available to all staff and organizations as a FREE resource. You can subscribe by going to www.BullyFreeAtWork.com and submitting your email address in the form on the right side of the page.

Bully Free At Work™: The Blog
(www.BullyFreeAtWork.com) has the top articles on workplace bullying, audio podcasts as well as the written transcripts if you prefer to read, and weekly posts that will keep you up to date and connected.

Our desire is to share the most relevant and well-researched information, and create inspiration and hope in order to move through the steps it takes to handle workplace bullying from both a personal point of view as well as an organizational point of view.